Shepherd & Sheep

Essays on Loving & Leading in a Local Church

shepherd & sheep

benjamin
vrbicek

FAN AND FLAME Press

Shepherd & Sheep: Essays on Loving & Leading in a Local Church

© 2021 Benjamin Vrbicek

A publication of FAN AND FLAME Press in Harrisburg, Pennsylvania

Editing: Alexandra Richter
Cover image: "The Good Shepherd," a woodcut image by Sebald Beham in 1527,
     adapted from the National Gallery of Art and used with permission
Cover & interior design: Benjamin Vrbicek

Paperback ISBN: 978-1-7348494-8-6
Ebook ISBN: 978-1-7348494-9-3

for Community Evangelical Free Church

Contents

PREFACE

Of all the apps on my phone, my favorite is Strava. It's the fitness tracker app I've used to log all my workouts for the last ten years. Every trip to the gym, every mile run on a road or a trail, and every mile ridden on a street or a stationary bike are all stored in my fitness history. With all that information, Strava creates what they call a "heatmap." Overlaid on a map of the world, Strava uses a system of colored lines with various thicknesses to show the areas an athlete has traveled most. The heatmap resembles a diagram of arteries and veins. My heatmap shows thick lines up the back of Blue Mountain Parkway in Harrisburg, Pennsylvania, a climb I've ridden well over one hundred times. It's a 1.59-mile climb to the top, with an average gradient of 8.4%, making it a Category 3 climb, although that probably only means something to cyclists. My quickest time was six years ago, which required just under eleven minutes of enjoyable suffering. I rarely check the leaderboard, but of the nearly two thousand attempts to summit the climb, that attempt is ranked forty-fifth. Not too bad.

A certain satisfaction comes not only from looking at individual excursions but also from seeing the aggregate of all the runs and all the rides in one place. Analyzing my heatmap, I notice the routines, those places and pathways I return to again and again. Some people might rather call these routines "ruts." But the difference of word choice between routines and ruts is more than the difference between "you say *to-may-toe*, and I say *to-mah-toe*." Ruts signify unthinking drudgery, a continuous grind from which we cannot pop loose. Routines signify, I like to think, the places my heart, and thus my feet, gravitate toward without much thinking. Routines signify the places we love to travel, even when we know doing so might involve eleven minutes of suffering. Or to say it in biblical language, where our routines are, there our treasure is also.

This summer my church graciously offered me a sabbatical after seven years together. The sabbatical plan had been in place for a long time, but with all the unrest in the world and in local churches, it seemed like following through with the sabbatical this summer might be unwise. Sometime in early winter, however, the Lord began to give our church a fresh supply of stability. So, when the time came, my church sent me away, and I left. I left to rest and read and write and exercise and date my wife and play with my children for fifteen weeks.

In the early weeks of my sabbatical, I happened to look over some of the essays I'd written while at our church. There are over three hundred on my blog and another seventy-five published elsewhere. Like analyzing my Strava heatmap, I began to notice routines, those themes I tend to return to again and again. I hadn't realized how often I alluded to *The Chronicles of Narnia* or how influential Zack Eswine's book *The Imperfect Pastor* has been to me. (Well, maybe I did know that one already.) As I looked over all the words, the largest cluster seemed to revolve around life in a local church, the relationship between pastors and parishioners, shepherds and sheep. That makes sense, of course; pastoring is, after all, my day job.

But pastoring a local church is far more than a job to me. The local church signifies the place my heart loves to be, even though I know being here will often involve more than eleven minutes of suffering. So, as a gift to our church and for the joy of collecting the best of the essays in one place, I put together this book, my writing heatmap, if you will. Perhaps a half dozen of these articles were first published on my website, but most of them appeared elsewhere, places such as Christianity Today, The Gospel Coalition, 9Marks, For The Church, Gospel-Centered Discipleship, and Desiring God. If you're interested, you can see the note at the end of the book for the details of where each entry was published.

I subtitled this collection *Essays on Loving and Leading in a Local Church* because I like to think the two go together: loving *and* leading, if not in my actual shepherding, at least as an aspiration. But I gave it the title *Shepherd & Sheep* as a way to remember that every shepherd is first and foremost a sheep in the fold of the Good Shepherd. As the apostle Peter shares, each local shepherd is an under shepherd of the chief Shepherd (1 Pet. 5:4). And praise God that the chief Shepherd loves the sheep he leads and leads the sheep he loves. Loving and leading go together with him.

May the congregational lives of local churches, the routines of local shepherds and sheep—our heatmaps—be to the praise of the glory of the Chief Shepherd's grace.

Benjamin Vrbicek
Harrisburg, Pennsylvania
Summer 2021

For thus says the LORD God: Behold, I, I myself will search for my sheep and will seek them out. As a shepherd seeks out his flock when he is among his sheep that have been scattered, so will I seek out my sheep, and I will rescue them from all places where they have been scattered on a day of clouds and thick darkness. And I will bring them out from the peoples and gather them from the countries, and will bring them into their own land. And I will feed them on the mountains of Israel, by the ravines, and in all the inhabited places of the country. I will feed them with good pasture, and on the mountain heights of Israel shall be their grazing land. There they shall lie down in good grazing land, and on rich pasture they shall feed on the mountains of Israel. I myself will be the shepherd of my sheep, and I myself will make them lie down, declares the LORD God. I will seek the lost, and I will bring back the strayed, and I will bind up the injured, and I will strengthen the weak, and the fat and the strong I will destroy. I will feed them in justice.

Ezekiel 34:11–16

BENDING THE COVID BOW OF BRONZE

One Pastor's Struggle toward Hope in God

Despite the numerical growth and spiritual maturity our congregation experienced, I presented my dilemma to the elder board. Something had to give. Now that I had been the lead teaching pastor for a while, I told them, I have learned one of two things: either I'm not called to pastoral ministry, or I'm doing it wrong. What other option could there be? I asked. Ministry should not be so hard.[1]

Calm and lovingly, the elder board listened. This meeting, by the way, was a month before most pastors had heard of the coronavirus.

At the time, I had just finished reading and resonated with what tennis legend Andre Agassi wrote in his transparent memoir *Open*.[2] Agassi tells of repeatedly hearing his gruff father bellow, "Hit harder, Andre!" as they practiced grueling hours on their backyard Las Vegas court. Seven-year-old Andre was

[1] This essay was first published by the Evangelical Free Church of America in May of the 2020, some ten weeks into the Covid pandemic.

[2] Andre Agassi, *Open: An Autobiography* (New York: Vintage, 2010).

forced to return balls shot out of a cannon he called "the dragon" until he grew to hate the sport that made him famous. And from his youth matches to winning Wimbledon, that voice in his head never stopped shouting. *Hit harder, Andre. Hit harder. Hit harder.*

I often hear voices telling me to try harder and do more, sometimes from the closest allies. In a recent Twitter thread about how pastors can serve their churches, one of my favorite authors said, "quarantine = overtime," adding that if a pastor thinks the quarantine means part-time, then he's "asleep at the wheel."

Okay fine, I mumble under my breath. I'm sure some pastor somewhere needed that salvo, just as Jeremiah needed to be chided about competing with horses and surviving in the thicket of the Jordan (Jer. 12:5). But what if a pastor feels drowsy at the wheel for reasons other than laziness? Sitting in the driver's seat nine months behind a short-staffed church has exhausted me—and that was *before* a global pandemic hit.

Between March and June, we are attempting twenty new or re-tooled ministry initiatives to serve our church during the crisis and prepare us for when we return. We're rebuilding our website, recording video sermons and worship songs, making phone calls to members and attendees, and posting daily Facebook videos throughout May.

Yet, for every three phone calls I make to church members, I feel guilty for not making ten. My theology tells me only the Chief Shepherd is omnipresent and omnipotent, but still I try to be everywhere at once, doing ministry fast and famously, as Zack Eswine critiqued in *The Imperfect Pastor*.[3] I hear Jesus

[3] Zack Eswine, *The Imperfect Pastor: Discovering Joy in Our Limitations through a Daily Apprenticeship with Jesus* (Wheaton: Crossway, 2015).

whisper that all who labor may come to him for rest. But for some reason my sin and psyche assume "all" can't include pastors; someone has to drive his sheep.

I know I'm not the only one who feels overworked. Our fridge holds a massive daily calendar to help coordinate the schedules of everyone in our large family. On day twenty-one of the lockdown, I stood behind my wife as she scratched a black X on the calendar. She looked at me and said, "That's sixty-three meals." We're now on day forty-five. Comedian Jim Gaffigan once said, "You know what it's like having a fourth kid? Imagine you're drowning, then someone hands you a baby."[4] We have six kids, and the older ones can eat more than me.

The Covid-era has also troubled my preaching. Most pastors had preaching classes in seminary where professors recorded sermons so we could analyze them post-op. Besides the theology of our messages, we'd break down goofy mannerisms like swaying side-to-side or verbal tics like saying "Umm." Whether a pastor has old VHS tapes in his basement, CD-ROMs in a desk drawer, or files on an Apple hard drive, I've never met a single one who enjoyed watching himself preach. It's the pits, actually.

Now, however, video preaching is all we can give our people. We toil each week over a text, preach the sermon to a camera, which hardly feels like preaching, and then email a link to our people, all the while feeling like, "I know, I know—I tried. I wish it were better too." Of course no members from our churches are so picky as to tell their pastor his eye contact is lousy, but we see all the imperfections in HD nonetheless. Preach harder. Preach harder. Preach harder.

---

[4] Jim Gaffigan, *Mr. Universe*, directed by Jay Karas (Chatsworth, California: Comedy Central Records, 2012), DVD.

*   *   *

The opening line of *The Voyage of the Dawn Treader* famously reads, "There was a boy called Eustace Clarence Scrubb, and he almost deserved it."[5] When I read my children *The Chronicles of Narnia*, I reserve a special voice for Eustace. I give him this rapid but whiny voice, like if Eeyore had too much coffee. My children love it.

But whenever I find myself telling a friend that life feels hard and I'm struggling to keep my head from drooping, I'm self-conscious my friend hears me in my Eustace voice. My ego disdains the thought of being perceived as a complainer, though I am not entirely sure why I fear this so intensely. My father loves me and never treated me like Agassi's father treated him. Yet somewhere along the way I adopted the view that sharing my struggles, however legitimate, can only be construed as complaining. *Rub some dirt in it, Benjamin.* How can a pastor complain when he still has his job and the financial giving to his church remains strong? Besides, all this craziness has caused people to reach out to God, some for the first time. Isn't this the stuff that wooed us into pastoral ministry in the first place— charging over dangerous hills waving the gospel banner?

A banker at our church tells of men crying on the phone because they recently lost their businesses—for good. Now, that is something worthy of complaint. Others have lost loved ones. Can I really mope about because I worked a few extra hours? Never mind that this race-like pace has continued at our church for nearly a year. *Don't be that guy,* I think. *John Piper found time to write a book during the lockdown.*

*   *   *

[5] C.S. Lewis, *The Voyage of the Dawn Treader*, The Complete Chronicles of Narnia (New York: Harper Collins, 1998), 293.

I enjoy writing and do it as often as my schedule allows, so I've wanted to write a helpful essay about our cultural Corona moment. Several organizations reached out to me for the same reason. Until now, I've baulked under the guise that people suffer from what I'll call "resource fatigue." It seems to me most Christian ministries have successfully scrambled to stuff the inboxes and social media feeds of their constituents, and I felt I had no compelling song to sing above the white noise.

But that is not the real reason I haven't written. I've resisted because I worry about what would happen if I wrote about my struggles without my verbal Instagram filter. Readers might schedule me for time with a counselor. And I might let them.

Maybe this is exactly where God wants me. Maybe squeezing the nub end of our fraying rope is where God wants you. Maybe he wants us here because, as Jared C. Wilson writes, "When you get to the end of your rope, there is Jesus."[6] Wilson doubles back over and over again to this theme of finding hope in God when all around our soul gives way. Maybe that's why I love Wilson's writing so much; it reminds me of Paul's comments about finding hope in God when we despair of life itself (2 Cor. 1:8–9).

"Until God is your only hope," he writes, "God will not be your only hope. Utter brokenness is key to gospel wakefulness, because we will not be all-satisfied in Christ until Christ is all we have."[7] This quote comes from a transparent section where Wilson describes a terrible season in life and marriage. He continues, "I was groaning in prayer in our guest room, flat on my face, wetting the carpet with tears the moment the Spirit

---

[6] Jared C. Wilson, *The Gospel According to Satan: Eight Lies about God that Sound Like the Truth* (Wheaton: Crossway, 2020), 84.

[7] Jared C. Wilson, *Gospel Wakefulness* (Wheaton: Crossway, 2011), 127.

whispered the gospel into my ear. That moment changed everything for me."[8]

Referencing this same, depression-filled season in another book, he writes, "It's my conviction that God will not become your only hope until he becomes your only hope."[9] Wilson writes something similar in his earlier book *Gospel Deeps*, my personal favorite in the Wilson corpus: "I realized that God would become my only hope when he had become my only hope."[10] Then, with the proverbial twinkle in his eye, Wilson adds, "Let the reader understand."

I *do* understand. And I'm coming to understand better. This is the Christian life—knowing the goodness and grace and sovereignty of God, and coming to know it deeper. It's like in the last chapter of Lewis's *The Last Battle*, when the faun named Tumnus says to Lucy, "The further up and the further in you go, the bigger everything gets. The inside is larger than the outside."[11] I finished reading the series to my family last week since the quarantine has given more evenings at home. Not all changes have been hard.

I have never been deployed as a soldier to a combat zone, a place where hostiles train to put bullets around your body armor and roadside bombs along your path. I don't know what it feels like to lie in bed worried for your actual life, so I don't want to cheapen the experience of deployment. But I can say there was a season a dozen years ago when I felt the way I imagined

---

[8] Ibid.

[9] Jared C. Wilson, *The Prodigal Church: A Gentle Manifesto against the Status Quo* (Wheaton: Crossway, 2015), 212.

[10] Jared C. Wilson, *Gospel Deeps: Reveling in the Excellencies of Jesus* (Wheaton: Crossway, 2012), 116.

[11] C.S. Lewis, *The Last Battle*, The Complete Chronicles of Narnia (New York: Harper Collins, 1998), 523.

pre-deployment might feel. I feared important relationships might break apart never to be put back together again, like glass dropped on hardwood.

This scary season came during the months leading up to when I would begin seminary full-time while also continuing to work nearly full-time to pay our bills. If you and I were sitting around a campfire, I could tell you all about that season, but here I'll keep it brief.

After I graduated from college, I did what most people hope to do: I found a job related to my degree in Mechanical Engineering. But I also knew and feared that God could call me back to school to someday deploy in pastoral ministry. Here was the crux of my fear: I had heard too many stories of students with their faith garbled up by the Christian academic machine. I also knew and feared my temperament, a twisted combination of the drive to excel and people please that always brought collateral damage even as it helped me overcome challenges.

When the day came to tell my engineering boss my plans to attend seminary and my desire to work for him part-time, with an annoyed look on his face, he said, "I'll think about it and get back to you." That conversation took place in early June, and school did not start until late-August. I wanted both of us to have plenty of time to prepare. I told my disappointed boss, "Thank you," and limped out of his corner office back to my cubicle.

I thought for sure he would fire me. No employee worked part-time where I worked, and certainly no one oscillated between full-time and part-time. Besides that, I was essentially asking him to keep investing in me for four more years even though I would eventually quit to take a job in ministry.

As the summer got hotter and the fall semester got closer, my boss didn't fire me. But neither did he tell me I could keep working. So I just kept showing up. Super awkward. Then August came, and so did my bill for classes. I paid, not sure whether I was dumb or full of faith. Still no answer from my boss.

Either the Spirit would whisper the gospel into my ear and God would become my only hope or I would whither.

As I laid in bed one night unable to sleep, worrying about my "deployment," I sensed God telling me to get up and pray. He generally doesn't do this sort of prodding with me, so I felt as confused as young Samuel. But I obeyed. "Speak, Lord, for your servant is listening." I sensed God direct me to the passage where David celebrates how God had trained King David's hands for war and helped him "bend a bow of bronze," as in a bow with arrows (2 Sam. 22:35 and Ps. 18:34).

As I understand it, no one knows if David hyperbolically meant an actual bow of bronze, thus a weapon humanly impossible to bend, or a bow reinforced with bronze, thus challenging to bend. The point preached the same way to my heart: God is our only hope when life feels difficult, even impossible.

Shortly after that night of prayer and right before seminary classes began, my boss called me into his office and said, "We can work this out." And we did. I worked for him during all of seminary. It was a tremendous blessing.

These same anxieties from a dozen years ago have crept back into my heart. I worry important relationships might break apart not to be put back together again. Maybe you feel this way too.

Ed Stetzer wrote about the recent, untimely death of Darrin Patrick, who was my pastor for several years when my wife and I were first married. On a Saturday morning over a breakfast of cheesy eggs and cubed potatoes in a St. Louis restaurant, Darrin encouraged me to try seminary at night for one year and then later go full-time during the day. Stetzer writes,

The truth is that pastors and leaders have daily struggles that are constantly pressing on them. This comes in the form of taking care of themselves spiritually, emotionally, and physically, as well as caring for their churches and staff they lead. Many also feel pressures from family and friends. And most carry burdens of others who confide in them to a degree that many of us cannot fathom.[12]

There might be another answer to my dilemma of either being not called to ministry or doing it wrong. Maybe ministry is just really hard.

And so maybe we don't need to hit harder, work harder, preach harder, pastor harder, or do anything else harder. Maybe, in the severe but sweet providence of God, the Covid-era will be the time we look back on, as David did, to say that the Lord made our feet like the feet of a deer and set us secure on the heights and trained our hands for war, so that our arms can bend a Covid bow of bronze. Let the reader and writer understand.

---

[12] Ed Stetzer, "Darrin Patrick's Death, His Love for Pastors, and How We Need One Another," *Christianity Today*, May 9, 2020, https://www.christianitytoday.com/edstetzer/2020/may/remembering-darrin-pastors-mental-health.html.

THE DAY THAT DARRIN DIED

Sadness over Darrin Patrick's Death

Last Friday I opened Twitter and saw the headline that pastor Darrin Patrick had died unexpectedly. Scrolling through my feed I saw pastor after pastor expressing surprise and sorrow. I felt the same. For several years, Darrin was my pastor. And although I haven't been a member of his church for many years, in a lingering way, I still felt as though he was one of my pastors—because pastors need pastors too.

Religious News reported that Darrin died from a self-inflicted gunshot.[1] You can read the article to get more background on his ministry influence, his rough patch a few years ago, and his return to what appeared to be healthy, pastoral ministry in a local church. I'm not going to write about all of that here, mostly because I only know those parts of his story the same way many of you do, that is, from a distance. Also,

[1] Bob Smietana, "Friends mourn Darrin Patrick, megachurch pastor and author, who died of apparent 'self-inflicted gunshot wound,'" *Religious News*, May 8, 2020, https://religionnews.com/2020/05/08/friends-mourn-darrin-patrick-mega church-pastor-and-author-who-died-unexpectedly/.

others have chronicled those events in more prominent places, as in Ed Stetzer's 2019 three-part series on Darrin's restoration process.[2] I'd like to stay more personal because that's all I know well, and also because one of Darrin's gifts was brevity. A long-winded reflection from me wouldn't honor that strength.

When my wife and I were first married, we moved to St. Louis. Darrin had planted The Journey only a few years before, and it was still relatively small in the summer of 2005. But the rapid growth had already begun or was about to begin in earnest. We followed The Journey's church moves and expansion across four different campuses in just two years, from Ladue to Brentwood to Tower Grove to West County. Our next move was to leave Darrin's church.

Shortly after we arrived at The Journey, I told Darrin I felt God calling me into pastoral ministry but struggled to work out the details of that call. He said we should grab breakfast. So, on a Saturday morning over plates of cheesy eggs and cubed potatoes at Stratton's Café, Darrin encouraged me to try seminary at night for one year and then later go full-time during the day. So I did.

I never had breakfast with Darrin again. That hurt. But it wasn't his fault or mine. There were a hundred, if not two hundred, young men just like me at The Journey preparing for ministry who wanted to learn from Darrin. He hadn't done anything wrong. It was just math. The parishioner-to-pastor ratio got skewed, more meeting requests than minutes in a day. So we left his church, not because we didn't love The Journey, but because I knew I needed to know a pastor and a pastor had to know me if I were going to be one someday. We found a small

---

[2] Ed Setzer, "A Pastor's Restoration Process: Journey to Healing Through the Eyes of Those Closest, Part 1: Darrin . . . Part 2: Amie . . . Part 3: Greg," *Christianity Today*, May 16–18, 2019, https://www.christianitytoday.com/edstetzer/2019/may/pastors-restoration-process-journey-to-healing-through-eyes.html.

church near our house where I knew a pastor and learned to pastor.

Although I didn't know Darrin well or for long, at significant moments in my life and ministry, I still wanted to give him updates. Sometimes I did. When I graduated from seminary and found my first job in pastoral ministry, I wrote him a long letter thanking him that some seventy-five months earlier he had encouraged me to pursue seminary; I finished strong and wanted Darrin to know I'd carried his counsel through. When Darrin spoke at the 2012 Desiring God conference, he saw me in the crowd, and we talked for several minutes before he spoke. When The Gospel Coalition published my first article, I sent the link to Darrin, which he seemed eager to read. Another time, I wrote a long, handwritten letter thanking him for specific lines from a sermon preached eight years before but remain words I'll never forget. A few years ago, he sent me a Twitter message asking me to apply for an opening they had at one of The Journey church campuses. I told him, Thanks but no.

In the best sense, Darrin was like a dad on a playground where lots of kids kept yelling, "Hey, look at me!" I was one of those kids. And I don't think that was bad. Paul writes to the church in Corinth that "though you have countless guides in Christ, you do not have many fathers" (1 Cor. 4:15). Darrin was a spiritual father to many.

On Friday when I saw the news about Darrin's death and received a few text messages, sadness ambushed me. Darrin had not been my pastor for nearly fifteen years, and yet, in another sense, through his writing and speaking ministry, he never really stopped being one of my pastors.

Until Friday.

"PASTOR, WHY AREN'T YOU PREACHING ABOUT WHAT'S HAPPENING?"

On Pastors and Pulpits and Current Events

In May of 2012, a sitting American President publicly and favorably addressed same-sex marriage for the very first time. I didn't mention this historic event in church the very next Sunday, or any Sunday for that matter.

A year or two after that particular event, I sat at a roundtable discussion with a dozen pastors. One of the leading pastors in our city told the rest of us that he had set aside his prepared sermon to address President Obama's remarks and instead talk about marriage. The way he relayed this detail more than implied, "All good pastors do the same," and I wasn't a good pastor.

I used to wonder if he was right.

This experience and many others like them get me thinking. Answering the one question of whether to address an event involves asking and answering many other questions.

If a pastor does address a current event, when should he do it? Should he address it with the church's weekly email and Facebook page? Addressing events this way allows us to do so outside of the regular worship service, which has advantages. But if the event should be addressed during the service, should this happen between worship songs, within the announcements, during the pastoral prayer, or in the sermon? And if during the sermon, how much time should it receive? A passing comment to show awareness or an in-depth analysis?

Here's another layer of complexity. Was the current event a national or global event, such as a hurricane, wildfire, shooting, or airplane crash, and thus not specifically related to your city? Or, is the current event a local one, such as the terrorist shooting around Christmas two years ago in Harrisburg, Pennsylvania where I live?[1] On a lighter note, when the Penn State football team wins their bowl game, should I mention that? (Some years I do and some I don't.)

Furthermore, pastors must consider timing. How soon should the event be addressed? For some events, waiting a week or more misses the opportunity. While for other events, waiting brings clarity.

Finally, who decides whether an event's importance justifies an address? I promise you that what some in my congregation consider important is not at all important to others. Some find the latest tweet from President Trump obnoxious, while others applaud it. And still others in my church don't know how to use "the Twitter." God loves us all and so do I.

These questions are not theoretical to me. Between one of our two worship services, a regular attendee placed his phone

---

[1] Jeremy Roebuck, "Was Harrisburg shooting spree a terror attack?" *Philadelphia Inquirer*, December 26, 2017, https://www.inquirer.com/philly/news/pennsylvania/was-harrisburg-shooting-spree-terror-attack-investigation-20171226.html.

in my hand to show me his social media feed. He wanted to know if his pastor knew if such and such an event had happened while we all slept the night before and whether I would address it during the second service because I failed to do so during the first. My friend's intentions were in the right place, but the second service began in forty-five seconds, and we still stood in the foyer. The event was not large enough that anyone else mentioned it to me. Right or wrong, I made the decision not to address the event in the second service. I wrestle with scenarios like this fifty times a year, especially in the wake of the coronavirus and George Floyd's death. I've probably used the word pandemic in my sermons three dozen times in the last few months.

If you are reading this and you're not a pastor, you probably have an opinion about what should be done in your church. Some people even leave churches and join others because of the way current events are addressed (or not addressed). So, let me ask, how do you arrive at an answer?

In the aftermath of the unrest in Charlottesville nearly three years ago, author Trevin Wax wrote a helpful article in which he said,

> On social media, multiple people counseled churches on how to respond the next morning. Some called for condemning white supremacy and Neo-Nazis by name. Others offered prayer for pastors who were revising their sermons or penning statements to read before the church. This sentiment popped up a few times: If your church doesn't address this tomorrow, find another congregation. The social media fever implied that failing

to speak on the issue indicated you were taking the side of white supremacists.[2]

Wax goes on to mention how his church addressed Charlottesville and offered several thoughtful questions he now uses as a filter in considering whether to address such events.

1.   Is this a history-making event that demands the church's immediate response?
2.   How "top of mind" or "close at hand" is the recent cultural event?
3.   Are you in danger of leading your church to be driven by current events?
4.   Are we in a cultural moment where the church's guidance may be necessary?[3]

These questions bring necessary clarity and, as much as possible, objectivity. I commend Wax's whole article to you.

Much more could be said than I've done so far. For example, I shouldn't fail to mention the necessity that everything said on Sundays be absolutely true. Christians shall not bear false witness, especially in a worship service. I can walk back or even repent of a tweet I hastily thumbed into cyberspace. But we must take vigilance that this is not needed for something said in a sermon.

When I was in seminary, the church we attended often had a children's sermon in the middle of the worship service. I distinctly remember a woman sharing with the children sitting at

[2] Trevin Wax, "When Should a Church Address a Current Event?" *The Gospel Coalition*, September, 5, 2017, https://www.thegospelcoalition.org/blogs/trevin-wax/when-should-a-church-address-a-current-event/.

[3] Ibid.

her feet the spiritual significance of each of the twelve days of Christmas and how the gospel connects allegorically to each day. The next week at church she told us how everything she taught the week before was wrong. An article making rounds on the Internet touched her heart, showed up prominently in our worship service, and then needed to be retracted. The congregation laughed at her *mea culpa*, her "oops—my bad." But this should not happen. "Not many of you should become teachers," writes James, "for you know that we who teach will be judged with greater strictness" (James 3:1).

Above, I mentioned an article about a shooting that took place in Harrisburg. But that article was published days later, and in it, *The Philadelphia Inquirer* still wrestled with whether to classify the shooting in our city as a terrorist act.

If you know for sure that a terrorist shooting happened in your city on Saturday, of course you mention it on Sunday. But question your epistemology. Before I say in a sermon that our city experienced an act of terrorism—or a hundred other things—I need to know for sure that we did. This level of assurance cannot be reached with a quick scroll through social media between services, which means I tend to be slow to speak and careful when I do (James 1:19). A media dogpile doesn't obligate me to jump too.

Let me come back to something Trevin Wax wrote in his article "When Should a Church Address a Current Event?" Wax believes the pastor-elder team at a church must evaluate whether their church is too driven by cultural events. It's not a hypothetical situation—if you don't ever ask the question, your church might be driven by the trends on CNN or Fox or Twitter more than you realize.

Some people, including some pastors, love to follow current

events the way a sports fan follows his or her team; staying current is both an enjoyable and meaningful hobby. They consume their favorite media outlet because they feel cultural awareness is essential but also because, let's be honest, it feels good to be in the know. There's nothing wrong with this, but the danger, as I see it, comes when Christians spiritualize interest in current events while not so subtly implying, "All good Christians do the same." As Trevin Wax writes, "In a given week, there is news from all over the world that could, in theory, swamp the service."[4] Indeed in our church of four hundred adults, most weeks some personal tragedy among us of one kind or another could swamp the service.

To lay my cards on the table, I'm not going to spend an hour before church every Sunday checking online to see what happened around the world while I slept. My time before church on Sunday mornings is best set aside for prayer, study, practicing my sermon, and meeting with a few people involved in the service. I don't have time (and don't plan to make time) each week before church to scour Fox News, CNN, and local news sources. When I wake up on Sundays, I switch my phone off "airplane mode" and skim my texts, emails, and personal social media feeds for a minute or two just to make sure a member of our church didn't die.

This intentional slowness is reinforced by another set of convictions at our church, namely, the commitment to expositional preaching. Most Sundays, we preach through one passage of Scripture. I won't argue expositional preaching is the only way to preach, but it means our church members don't arrive with the expectation we'll address the latest cultural holiday, election result, hurricane, shooting, or some other tragedy.

[4] Wax, "When Should a Church Address a Current Event?" *The Gospel Coalition*.

When the riots happened in Charlottesville that prompted Wax's article—which feels like a long time ago now and highlights the ephemeral nature of many but not all current events—our worship leader led us in a corporate reading of a psalm of lament, and I weaved a few relevant comments into my sermon. But most of the time when we address an event, we try to do it as naturally as possible, which means it needs to arise from the text of Scripture we are preaching that week. And if it doesn't, we don't force it.

After Floyd's death—which, for a host of reasons, captured public attention across the world—our church focused the whole Sunday service toward longing and lament, even adjusting the sermon text to better fit the occasion. Some complained we went too far and others that we didn't say enough. This month, we have planned two nights of teaching and discussion at our church with our best leaders speaking about grace and race and to where the church, even in our particular church, has fallen short and what hope the gospel extends amid all the unrest.

If you're the teaching pastor, you don't have to make these calls alone. Send a group text to the other elders of your church the day before. Let them weigh in. Back in January our church acknowledged Sanctity of Human Life Sunday but only after the elders of our church vetted the flyer provided to us by the local Crises Pregnancy Center. Wording always matters, and a team of leaders looking over messaging, to use a marketing word, is especially important when gospel winsomeness on certain flashpoint issues has been often overlooked, as with abortion.

As culture becomes less and less familiar with Christianity and the Scriptures, the people in our churches will need more and more help connecting the events around them to a Christian worldview. I don't want to underappreciate this critical aspect of discipleship. Elder-qualified teaching pastors are far more competent to interpret cultural events from a biblical worldview than any secular news outlet.

Therefore, I concede the point that no dichotomy exists between the superiority of Jesus and a discussion of current events. Paul writes of Christ's preeminence as the head of the body and as the firstborn from the dead (Col. 1:18), so there must be a way of discipleship that can discuss current events while displaying the reign of King Jesus, not obscuring it. John Piper's recent book *Coronavirus and Christ* is a good example of theological exposition that exalts the supremacy of Jesus and also engages with the questions of a cultural moment.[5]

But still, if every drone strike, vote about minimum wage, or sexual abuse story must become a Sunday conversation in your local church, then I fear all our effort to make fully-formed disciples of Christ will remain reactive rather than proactive; what we preach about will be constantly dictated to us—sometimes on short notice—rather than prayerful pastors being carried along by the Holy Spirit.

Undoubtedly some in our church take our leadership's lack of frequent and persistent addressing of current events as though we are cowardly avoiding risk, or that we are monks retreating from culture, or that we are ostriches with our heads in the sand.

I don't think such criticisms are valid. Really, we're trying to give people a gift—whether they see it that way or not. Fifty-two Sundays a year, we seek to remind our people of an easily forgotten truth.

---

[5] John Piper, *Coronavirus and Christ* (Wheaton: Crossway, 2020).

In a world enamored with whatever seems most urgent, even Christians can lose sight of what's truly important and lasting. The word of God, while it speaks to every aspect of our lives in every moment of our lives, will also outlast every personal, local, national, and global crisis.

If the Lord does not come back beforehand, the blood spilled on Little Roundtop will one day be remembered the way we remember Caesar crossing the Rubicon. One day the monuments of Washington DC will become ruins like the Roman Colosseum. And when pastors major on the urgent, we can inadvertently lead people to forget that "the word of our God will stand forever" (Isa. 40:8). It's this reminder above all else—the reminder of the endurance of the word, the finitude of man, the transcendence of God, the assurance of a final judgment to right all wrongs, and the amazing grace of Jesus—that I want to give our people each Sunday. Those who know they stand upon a rock stand strongest in a storm.

4

REDEEMING PASTORAL AMBITION

On Seeking (and Not Seeking) Great Things for Oneself

Forest fires rage each year in California and Arizona in the summer consuming everything in their path. Saplings as new as the spring and mature trees as old as the Declaration of Independence are scorched to ash. Too often, our desire for greatness is like that—an all-consuming fire.

The Bible recounts story after story of men and women who sought their own greatness. We see this in godless rulers such as Pharaoh in the book of Exodus and Nebuchadnezzar in the book of Daniel. Sometimes we see worldly glory seekers among the faithful, like when God rebuked Jeremiah's trusted scribe, saying, "And do you seek great things for yourself? Seek them not" (Jer. 45:5).

Yet the quest for glory still rages. Incalculable amounts of exertion, passion, money, and skill are employed in the pursuit. If we could know our own hearts perfectly, we'd have to admit that this is our story too. Some vision of greatness, whether consciously or not, tugs us along. It seems to be the subject of every commencement speech. "Go change the world," ambitious graduates are told, which usually means, "Go become great in the eyes of the world." Our current culture of side-hustles can stoke discontentment too; at times I've struggled to feel like my calling to pastor a local church is enough, as though if I did more then I'd be something more worthwhile. If I were a pastor-author or pastor-speaker or pastor-entrepreneur or pastor-whatever, *then* I'd have meaning. I'm probably not the only pastor who feels this way.

The disciples of Jesus had this same problem. In Mark 9, after beholding the glory of their Lord in his transfiguration, Mark tells us the disciples engaged in quite possibly the dumbest argument in the history of the world: the fight about which of the disciples was the greatest.

The context of the conversation is what makes it so ridiculous. Consider what happened in Mark 9. Jesus revealed his glory on the mountain, showing he's not weak and feeble but strong and glorious. Jesus then received the stamp of approval from God the Father and was highlighted as far more important than Moses and Elijah, two significant Old Testament prophets. Then Jesus victoriously battled a demon which had previously defeated the disciples. Then Jesus promised to rise from the dead, invoking imagery of himself as the exalted "Son of Man" figure mentioned in Daniel 7:9–14. The grossly understated takeaway from Mark 9 is that Jesus is a big deal.

When Jesus asks the disciples what they discussed, Mark says they kept silent because "on the way they had argued with one another about who was the greatest" (9:34). They won't answer because of shame. They've got hands in the cookie jar but reckon that if they slide the jar behind someone's back, well, maybe Jesus won't know.

But he knows. He sees the crumbs on the floor and the chocolate on their cheeks. Their petty and myopic argument about worldly greatness is sin, just like when we pastors size each other up at conferences and seminary students view classmates as competitors.

When I attended a pastor's conference recently, I dreaded others saying, "So, tell me about your church." First, I'm leery of using the pronoun "my" when speaking about the church I pastor because I know how much my heart would love to consider it that way—mine. Perhaps there's an analogy we could make to the phrase "Lord willing" (James 4:13–15). We don't have to add the phrase to everything we say. The biblical authors didn't. But that we consider our plans in subjection to the Lord's will should always be understood even when left unstated. In the same way, when we say "my church" we must always know it's Jesus who builds *his* church; he doesn't build ours (Matt. 16:18). Second, when people ask about my church, even when the person means something warm and amiable, I worry my answer devolves into the verbal equivalent of strutting a catwalk in my swimsuit while others hold up a scorecard. It's as unattractive as it sounds.

Author and pastor Zack Eswine writes about ambition as having a certain "arson" to it in his wonderful book *The Imperfect Pastor*.[1] That's certainly true. But if we read Jesus's words carefully, we'll see Jesus doesn't want to put the fire out. He wants to douse our desire for greatness with gasoline. That's a provocative statement and one open to misunderstanding, but it seems to be the lesson Peter and the other disciples learned when they came down the mountain in Mark 9.

And what makes the lesson so remarkable is that you might expect Jesus to issue a harsh rebuke. I mean, he is a prophet,

[1] Eswine, *The Imperfect Pastor*, 19.

and prophets do that sort of thing from time to time. Instead what they got—and what we get—is extreme patience. He teaches; he instructs; he redefines; he redirects. We would fire these disciples and hire others. But Jesus loves them. In verse 35 we read that he sat down and called the twelve to himself. Then he told them, "If anyone would be first, he must be last of all and servant of all." Notice the exact phrasing: "servant of all," not just servant of the greats, like servant of a famous pastor or a seminary president. His point is that the greatness of our service is enhanced not diminished by the lack of greatness of those we serve.

For us visual learners, Jesus goes on to illustrate his point. He called a child to himself, took the child in his arms, and said to the disciples, "Whoever receives one such child in my name receives me, and whoever receives me, receives not me but him who sent me" (9:37). Jesus implies that greatness is receiving children because they are a specific example of the broader principle of servanthood. In receiving children, Jesus shows us that true greatness—by his definition—is serving, loving, and caring for the needs of people who cannot repay you.

This might not come as a shock to you, but the disciples don't get it—not before the cross and resurrection, anyway. As Luke records it, even during the last supper with Jesus, this same argument flared among them. "And he took a cup, and when he had given thanks he said, 'Take this, and divide it among yourselves. . . . A dispute also arose among them, as to which of them was to be regarded as the greatest" (Luke 22:17, 24).

The lessons about true greatness didn't stick because we need more than a lesson and an invitation. We need redemption. Our definition of greatness is too corrupt. We all have in us what comedian Brian Regan calls the "me-monster." I *give away 20% of my income. I memorized the book of Ephesians. I have 2,000 Facebook friends. My church had a dozen baptisms last month. I bench press 350 lbs. and run marathons. I . . . I . . . I . . .*

Jesus told his disciples, "I am among you as the one who serves" (Luke 22:27). Indeed he was. And his service to sinners leads him to the cross where he dies for our sins, including those we commit pursuing greatness in the eyes of the world. And he redeems our corruption and shows us the better way. If you want to change the world, have the ultimate side-hustle, and be a modern prince of preachers, then by the grace of God be a servant of all. It's when the fire of your ambition burns brightest for God's glory, not your own, that your life will bless others rather than consume everything in its path.

5

SPRING LOADED CAMMING DEVICES AND THE EXPOSITORY SERMON

What Rock-Climbing Gear Has to Do with Preaching

Picture yourself rock climbing. The sun shines and sweat drips from your forehead. You're fifty feet above the ground on the side of a rockface. Your arms burn. You keep dipping your sweaty hands in the bag of chalk that hangs from your belt as though that will make climbing easier. Of course, you expect some measure of difficulty—you're rock climbing after all. But when your pulse begins to climb too high, you pause for a moment to catch your breath. For the first time you glance down. Woah—*it's a long way to the bottom.*

But then, as you reach for the next handhold, your right hand slips off the rock. *Oops,* you think.

Suddenly your right foot slips too. *Double oops!*

Now you cling with only your left hand and left foot; your body swings out from the rockface like a barn door on hinges. Your thoughts flash to the last anchor you set in the rock. *How well did I place it? Will it hold me if I fall?*

This situation is a lot like life. You are working hard and go about your days with some sweat on your forehead, or at least under your arms. The kids get the flu, work requires overtime, and drama flares up with your in-laws. But you expect these sorts of difficulties and take them in stride.

Then the CFO of your company announces a plan to "re-organize." Your job, your income, your livelihood slips away. It's *fine*, you think. *I can deal. I'm still holding strong.* But then your wife says, "Honey, I think I found a lump on my breast." Now both a foot and hand have slipped off the rockface, and you barely hold it together. Your body swings like a door on hinges dangling above danger. *Woah, it's a long way down.*

As a teaching pastor, I think about these types of situations often. And not only has rock climbing become a helpful metaphor for the way I consider life, it's become a helpful metaphor for something I try to accomplish in my preaching.

But let me back up for a moment.

There are two main ways to rock climb. Well, I suppose there is a third way, the way of Alex Honnold free soloing up El Capitan, but let's not count that as a way others should imitate. The first way I have in mind requires using "spring loaded camming devices," or just "cams" for short. When you climb with cams, you wedge your own anchors in the rock as you climb up the rockface or you use anchors previously placed by others. They call this type of climbing *lead* rope climbing, as opposed to *top* rope climbing. In top rope climbing, your harness is attached to a rope that is looped through an anchor at the top of the climb, hence the name. However, when you climb using cams (lead rope climbing), there's no anchor fixed at the top of the climb; there are only the cams placed in the rock as you climb your way to the top.

Therefore, in the event of a fall while lead rope climbing with cams, you don't need a dozen superficial anchors. Each anchor must count. Each anchor must be firm and deep into the rock. A chintzy fastener casually placed won't do the job; it won't take the force of an unexpected fall. Anchors improperly set, even if you have a dozen placed every two feet, will pop pop pop under the weight of your fall. Instead, you need just one quality cam wedged into a crevice. Just one cam will hold you when you fall, that is, if it's properly set.

For me, rock climbing with cams is a metaphor for preaching. Too often in sermon preparation I feel the pressure to say everything about everything. But there is only so much time in any given sermon, and a dozen random comments—all true enough—are like chintzy fasteners. They simply won't hold when hardships cause our faith to slip.

Instead, I want my preaching each week to set just one anchor deep into some aspect of who God is and what he has done, is doing, and will do for us in Christ. People on the face of a rock, people who could lose their grip at any moment, need the stability offered in gospel preaching. I need this in my life too.

Don't misunderstand me, though. I know sermons do not save people or keep us saved any more than a cam by itself keeps climbers safe. But what that anchor *can* do, and what a sermon *should* do, is keep people firmly attached to the rock, or in my metaphor, The Rock. Stability and joy and life are offered to those securely attached to the rock.

Implications of this metaphor extend to how we organize our worship services, attempting to link the themes of sermons and the themes of our liturgy and song. Additionally, consider how this metaphor might challenge Christians to attend church with greater frequency; if you miss chances to insert anchors, you might fall a dozen or two dozen feet before you stop, which breaks bones.

But I want to zero in on preaching. This metaphor is a large part of why I favor the type of sermons we call "expository." Expository is a term preachers use from time to time, but we rarely explain what we mean by this term. At *The Gospel Coalition's* 2011 National Conference, in one of the panel discussions there was a great conversation about preaching generally and the expository sermon specifically. In that discussion, Pastor Mark Dever succinctly described expository sermons like this: "In expository sermons, the main point of the Scripture passage is the main point of the sermon."[1]

That's simple enough. I like that definition: the one main point of the sermon comes from the same one main point of the Scripture passage. To me, that definition sounds remarkably similar to what I mean when I say that each week's sermon should put just one anchor in The Rock—deeply and properly.

Don't hear what I'm not saying. I'm not saying a topical sermon is inherently a chintzy anchor. If you ask me, when done well, a topical sermon has the potential to affix our hearts more deeply to an aspect of the gospel than an average expository sermon. But to also be candid, I don't have the ability to preach deep topical messages week in and week out. I find preaching good topical sermons overwhelming, and I also find them disconnected from the way most Christians read their Bibles.

I realize that many of the people who might read this essay are not preaching pastors. However, perhaps you occasionally have the opportunity to lead a Bible study of one kind or another. I'd encourage you to consider how "making the main idea

[1] Crawford Loritts, Mark Dever, and Tim Keller, "What Should a Local Church Look Like?" *The Gospel Coalition*, May 23, 2010, http://resources.thegospel coalition.org/library/what-should-a-local-church-look-like-en.

of the Bible passage, the main idea of your lesson" might strengthen your lesson by giving your lesson focus.

This isn't the place for describing all of the tools pastors use to find the main point of a passage. How to find the main point of a passage in light of what God has done for us in Christ would require another essay. But once I find the main point of a passage, my next steps in sermon preparation attempt to mold every aspect of the sermon—the outline, the explanations, the illustrations, the applications, and so on—to serve this one end, that is, serve the main gospel point of the passage. When you and I do that as we teach, I think we can rightly call our lessons and sermons "expository."

And when we teach the gospel like this week in and week out, we will provide our people with firm and deep anchors to the only Rock who can save us.

6

WHEN MY CHURCH WAS
WASHED WITH BUTTER

Reflections on the One-Year Anniversary of Covid Shutdowns

The very weekend before our church shut down last year, we hired a new associate pastor. Spirits were high among our members, and momentum—not sorrows—like sea billows rolled.

A year later, we have more church services, not to pack vibrant, bustling crowds into our sanctuary. I coated half of our pews with blue painter's tape to block entrance to the rows; we added services to get smaller and more distant. Our pastors, staff, and volunteers work harder to seemingly accomplish less. The pastors of your church probably do too.

As we approach the anniversary of a full year since the beginning of all the various iterations of Covid-church, I lament the many losses of connection and normalcy, along with lamenting missing sheep, masked services, video preaching, Zoom Sunday School, and the like. I understand it all, but I lament it—as we should.

*   *   *

In short, I miss the days when my church was washed in butter. This allusion comes from Job's lamentations over the loss of his former blessings. "Oh," he says, "when my steps were washed with butter" (Job 29:2, 6), the time before sorrows like sea billows rolled.

Maybe this butter metaphor has so captivated me because seven years ago the Lord took away my ability to eat dairy. God did not give me a dollop of lactose intolerance but an allergic gut-punch that often results in days of crushing sickness. And here Job, bless his heart, longs for the days when the cream and the fat and the buttery goodness of the Lord oozed all around him. Thus, Eugene Peterson paraphrases the opening lines from this chapter as Job's longing for "the good old days" (The Message).

But the emotion driving Job's laments is not just sadness over the loss of his extravagant prosperity, what we might call lament for the loss of *mere* prosperity. Job lost something virtuous, well-rounded, and Godward. He laments the loss of the days when he caused the "widow's heart to sing" (v. 13). He misses the days when he "broke the fangs of the unrighteous" (v. 17). He weeps for the time "when [his] children were all around [him]" (v. 5)—the ten children he and his wife buried in ten coffins on the same day. And chiefly Job laments the days when he felt "God watched over [him]" (v. 2).

I asked my family what they missed from church before Covid. My oldest son said with no hesitation, "The hot chocolate." Another daughter rejoined, "And powdery donuts."

These may feel inconsequential in the scheme of things, like melodramatic lament for a stubbed pinky toe. But pastor's kids lamenting the loss of Sunday morning snacks is indicative of greater loss. Our church café, formerly a place of fellowship and prayers and hugs and laughter and bustling crowds, now has a cloudy plastic tarp draped across the coffee carafes. When we covered our coffee and hot chocolate, we thought it might keep dust off for the few weeks they would go unused. They've now remained covered and unused for 52 weeks.

And not only do my children miss the snacks, so do the children of the many refugees and immigrants who call our church home. Throughout the week our lives might not overlap as much as they should, but we're all one at the foot of the cross and a box of pastries. Even our church cleaner tells me she misses the day when the café had crumbs everywhere on Monday morning.

My wife said she missed seeing the offering collected. We used to pass the plate in worship services because we saw it as worship. Now, if people want to give, we direct them to impersonal decorative boxes screwed to the wall by the exterior doors. "Have a nice week; don't forget to give."

If I were to tell you what I miss as a pastor, I'd need more words than Job used in chapter 29.

Yet the hand of the Lord still rests upon our church, as it did on Job. Even when our cups do not runneth over, God sits with us in the ashes.

Our church attempted all the options: online, in-person with and without masks, less singing, more singing, and so on. Some of the sweetest times in the last year were our outdoor services. They allowed our more Covid cautious members to worship in the same services as, shall we say, our less Covid cautious members.

But we almost didn't even try outdoor services. Back on a rainy day in May, a few of our leaders "mocked up" the front yard of our church with chairs. "I think we can get seventy-five seats in our front yard," we said to each other. Because we're tucked into a neighborhood, we wrote letters to nearby homes assuring them we'd not use any amplification for music or preaching. I didn't think preaching Christ with a megaphone would help our neighbors fall in love with him. So we didn't. By the end of the summer, there weren't seventy-five people spread out together. I had to yell to the back of a lawn filled with two-hundred and fifty people. Each Sunday I came home soaked in sweat but so pleased to pretend to be Whitefield.

The outdoor services often brought humor. Once, in the middle of a sermon, a guy putted by on a motorized scooter blaring music from a boom box bungeed to his handlebars. At full blast Marvin Gaye serenaded us with "Sexual Healing."

God also used Covid to change me as a leader, though it's been more of a death and resurrection, really. More than once I felt myself standing on the edge of quitting pastoral ministry with toes peeking over the ledge. My wife told me, bless her heart, not in so many words, "Let's curse God and die."

We don't feel on the edge now. I had to change, or better, parts of me—like grains of wheat falling to the ground—did have to die. In hindsight I see how aspects of my ministry, identity, and idolatry had braided together in a tight three-cord strand. In the ashes, God scraped away my sin with broken pottery. "It hurt worse than anything I've ever felt," said Eustace Scrubb. But we endure it for "the pleasure of feeling the stuff peel off."[1]

---

[1] C.S. Lewis, *The Voyage of the Dawntreader*, The Complete Chronicles of Narnia (New York: Harper Collins, 1998), 326.

I certainly lament the loss of the good ol' days, the days before Covid, the days when our churches were washed with cream and the buttery goodness of the Lord oozed all around us.

Yet the eyes of faith tell me those days are still today.

7

MINISTRY MORNING, NOON, AND NIGHT

A Day in the Life of a Pastor

"I will most gladly spend and be spent for your souls."
— The Apostle Paul

Sometimes people tease me that pastors only work one day a week. Sometimes they are not teasing.

The last time I saw my grandpa alive, he was one of them. "What does a pastor do all week anyway? You only work like one hour." I wanted to tell him our church has three worship services on Sunday morning, and they go four hours by themselves, and I get there long before we open and stay long after we've closed. But that response has too much snark.

Really, I wanted to tell him this.

Morning

I wake at 4:45 am to the muted vibrating of my iPhone. The phone rests on my nightstand on top of a book and a hand towel because the extra padding dulls the noise: phones on wooden nightstands that vibrate two hours before first light do not make for happy marriages. I know from experience.

By 5:00 I am on my living room couch to read through the three chapters of the book of Nahum, a book that ends with a provocative question. "All who hear the news about you clap their hands at your fall, for who has not felt your endless cruelty?" the prophet asks concerning the ancient Assyrian city of Nineveh. I read this, and I am reminded of a little Bible trivia. Only the book of Jonah also ends with a question, which also happens to be a book about Nineveh.

Each year I try to trek from cover to cover. Some mornings a verse or phrase sparks deeper joy in God. Some mornings a verse or phrase sparks conviction of sin and a deeper understanding of my need for Jesus. This morning, like a lot of them, the sparks do not fly, my eyelids droop, and I wish I had mined more from God's word than trivia factoids.

After I put Nahum away I open my laptop to edit a friend's book proposal, the business plan for an unwritten and unpublished book that dreams of someday hitting Amazon and blessing readers—and maybe the author. I know something of these dreams. I told my friend I would do this yesterday, but I ate something at dinner two nights ago that left me too sick yesterday morning to get up early and write. Today, however, I feel great; food allergies strike randomly like that.

At 6:44 I email my friend who lives in London his book proposal. A few hours later he tells me thank you and that "the feedback was spot-on," which is nice to hear but is tempered with the knowledge that no traditional publisher has ever found my own book proposals spot-on.

I eat breakfast around the table at 7:00 with my wife and six children. This morning Brooke made toasted bagels and turkey sausage links. We all talk about our day. For three minutes I also read a children's Bible based on the book of Acts as I wonder to myself if I try to cram too much into the morning. We have never read anything as a family at breakfast, and maybe we shouldn't.

Breakfast ends with my toddler yelling from the bathroom potty for my wife to come help. I help instead of her because my wife does it all the time and taking my turn makes me feel like an "Ephesians 5" type of husband even though I know I've domesticated the idea of a husband loving his wife as Christ loved the church, giving himself up for her.

Once we've walked our children to the bus stop and back, I shower quickly and make the three-minute commute to work. But my wife calls me on the way to tell me I forgot my laptop, so I go back quickly to grab it. "Quick" starts to feel like the key word of the day.

When I make it to church, I record a nine-minute sample section of an audiobook in the church basement before the rest of the staff arrives. I wanted to get the recording done before my true workday starts. I made the sample to figure out if the equipment I own can reach professional-grade quality. I sort of doubt it will; I used a bunch of winter blankets from my house to make a fort to dampen ambient sound, which sure didn't make me feel much like a professional.

Now the day picks up. I answer emails and read a chapter of a book about the gospel by Ray Ortlund. At noon, a man will come to talk about the chapter because he will lead our small group Bible study through the material this coming Sunday night. The study this week engages with Galatians 2. How exactly in 2:4, we wonder, did false brothers slip in to spy out their freedom in Christ [*not* to be circumcised]? This required strange spycraft. And the "circumcision party" (2:12), we think, does not sound much like a party. I hold my fist to my mouth and make a kazoo noise. We both chuckle. He is a newer Christian, and this will be his first time leading. Just two years ago was the first time he had ever been to a small group Bible study. Aslan, as they say, is on the move.

Noon

But before my friend can meet in the church café, I walk in the rain holding an umbrella. With another staff member I visit a neighbor who will likely die in the next day or two. We walk down the alley behind church, make a right on Ash Street, then a left to pass by a dozen houses. We shake and collapse our umbrellas, knock, and see if someone answers. The wife of the dying man sent the church a note through our Facebook page. I saw her message as I set my wakeup alarm right before I crashed but did not respond; I knew I would just show up when I could. She had also messaged us eight weeks ago when they first got the news her husband was dying.

"The doctors gave him three to six weeks, and here we are at week eight," she says to us while I sit next to the metal gurney bed placed in their living room. He lays on the bed with his eyes closed and breathes heavily. The bed, like death, does not belong in the living room. "He wanted to beat the doctor's six-week prediction," she tells us, "and live to vote one more time." He did both.

But when we visited eight weeks ago, we all sang acapella about peace like a river and listened to this child of God, who looked so healthy, tell stories of how God saved him and called him into prison ministry. He also told us of his love for birds. On this visit he tells no stories as sorrows like sea billows roll. The morphine has already induced sedation. Although his bed sits by the window to see his bird feeders, the blinds are pulled shut. Together we pray with his soon-to-be widow and wipe our sniffles away from behind our disposable masks. I stand up, pat his legs, and tell him he has run a great race and God will carry him home. He opens his eyes and speaks his last words to me. "I'm just so gassed." I say back, "God will carry you." We leave in the rain and walk back up the street and alley to our office.

More meetings in the afternoon. First, a team of four offers critiques of the merits of my sermon from the previous Sunday on John 4, the thirsty woman who had five husbands, and our culture's schizophrenic view of sex—sex means everything and nothing at the same time. Not my best sermon, we all agree, but still good. I probably should have talked more directly to our broken sexualities rather than around the topics, they suggest.

Then we have a staff meeting, which assigned me a few action items I quickly knock out so that I can have more time to call a husband. This husband had asked me to talk a while ago, but I could not make time for him—and I have felt bad about that. But now we talk, and I hear more about his marriage, which we have discussed several times before. I hang up the phone and contemplate that today I had prayed with a man on hospice and now pray with a man whose marriage might as well be on hospice. The marriage might recover, but we sort of doubt it. The morphine of lawyers and legal separation, as it were, has put the marriage in sedation. I fear it is only a matter of time before it passes. Only God knows.

Surprised I finished my office day before 4:00, I realize I can squeeze in a quick trip to the gym, so I do. Someone going through our church membership class raised questions about our eschatology and had emailed me a sermon by David Jeremiah. I could not make time to watch the sermon last week or the week before, so I play the sermon about the end times on YouTube at the gym while I do a CrossFit workout. The workout involves alternating between the rowing machine and throwing a twenty-pound rubber ball ten feet in the air. I like our new member and believe he likes our church, but I wonder if he noticed the sermon said my view of the return of Christ did not take the Bible seriously. Maybe he did notice and sent it for that reason.

I make a quick trip home from the gym so I can make the most of my quick hour at home to talk with my wife and kids before I go back to work. I sit at the table and read a chapter of *The Magician's Nephew* with one of my daughters. We don't finish the chapter before I have to shower quickly and scoot back to work.

And Night

I'm in the church basement again—this time a different room. I sit in a circle of chairs with our team of pastor-elders. Most elder meetings we laugh and pray and discuss how best to lead our church. Tonight is no different. But we also wrestled with more church discipline cases than usual. Again, Aslan is on the move—but sometimes his movement makes life messy.

Before I leave the church, I bump into a friend who talks to me about his recent engagement and asks if I would officiate his wedding and oversee his premarital counseling. Delighted he asked, I say yes.

Now I sit at home on the couch eating dairy-free chocolate chip cookies I just slathered with chilled Pillsbury vanilla frosting as I talk to my wife about the day—but only after I made a quick round to all my children's bedrooms to say goodnight. They were already in bed but waiting up for Dad.

My wife and I sit and talk about the day and the pastor-elder meeting. She knew enough of the items on the agenda to know we should talk for a bit. It is too late in the evening, but we start the next episode in our current Netflix series anyway: season 3, episode 4 of *The Walking Dead*. Then we brush our teeth, and I set my alarm, turn down my ringer volume, toggle on airplane mode, and place the phone on the nightstand.

I kiss my wife, and in the last thirty seconds before I fall asleep, I think to myself that pastors do not only work one day a week. We must work at least two.

Before my grandpa died, he wrote me a short letter of apology for when he had mocked pastors, for when he had mocked me. The apology made officiating his funeral easier.

Annie Dillard wrote, "How we spend our days is, of course, how we spend our lives. What we do with this hour, and that one, is what we are doing."[1] If "this hour" and "that one" were less full than they were today and more balanced, that might be more ideal and more sustainable. But I do believe that if we pastors spend our days thus, we spend our lives well.

---

[1] Annie Dillard, *The Writing Life* (Harper Perennial, 2013), 32.

8

WAS I BETRAYING MY CHURCH BY INTERVIEWING ELSEWHERE?

The Conflicting Season of a Pastoral Transition

While visiting the elders of another church to learn about a pastoral opening, I felt like the main character in *Alexander and the Terrible, Horrible, No Good, Very Bad Day*.

Terrible turbulence required not one but two attempts to land at Dulles. But I only learned that after we deplaned. Woofing my cookies kept me too busy to notice. Next was the horrible cab ride, which involved 90 minutes of stop-and-go traffic to the outskirts of Washington, DC in record-breaking heat.

Because of these delays, the elders and I scrambled to coordinate a new meeting location by phone. We chose a gas station in some suburb of DC for the pickup. I had 15 minutes to change from travel clothes to something nicer before the search team picked me up, so I got the key to use the restroom around back. I've never been one to quickly label a moment "spiritual warfare," but as I struggled to button my dress shirt, I was ready to rebuke the flickering fluorescent light that compounded my acute nausea.

Yet this prelude to our meeting wasn't the most difficult part. The worst part was shaking hands with the elders, feeling like a traitor to my current church. Under cover of darkness, my meeting wasn't just dinner and drinks with new friends; it was treason.

Or perhaps not. If God is the one calling a pastor from one church to another, there must be a way for that transition to proceed in a God-honoring manner, right? And surely a transition that honors the Lord will also respect the churches involved, as well as a pastor's family. Still, I couldn't help feeling that my clandestine visit made me guilty of treachery.

Back at the church I pastored, I sat in staff meetings planning the church's future while knowing my own future might be elsewhere. I tried to soften the certainty of plans, giving vague answers about my participation or a project's timeline. That made me feel worse and probably confused others. I wanted to let my yes be yes, but I didn't always know how. Besides the guilt of knowing I might leave, I felt an abiding loneliness. My wife and I told only our two closest friends that we were considering a move. No one else knew. I remember doing a video conference interview in my living room while my wife took our children to a McDonald's PlayPlace—even my children couldn't know. In hindsight, I wish I had been more open with my senior pastor. I was an associate at the time. Not every pastor can trust their church leadership with such information, but I think I could have.

Even when a pastor feels confident it's the right time to leave, there isn't a perfect way to share that news with people. Feelings will be hurt no matter how thoughtful and truthful the pastor tries to be.

Eventually, in my own transition process, I concluded it was time to leave. When I told one man I would be leaving, he asked what Bible verses had been particularly instructive as I contemplated the transition, what "word from the Lord" led me to this decision. I couldn't cite a specific verse, which disappointed him. He wanted me to speak of my departure in more spiritual terms. Another man on staff detested the over-spiritualization of decisions—using Christianese like "God's calling" and "open doors"—when sometimes decisions are as fleshly as a lust for greener grass. How could I talk about my departure in a way that would satisfy both of these individuals?

I don't think my transition was the sinful act of chasing after a better pastorate or a cowardly running from responsibilities in my current one, but I sympathize with my coworker's aversion to over-spiritualizing big decisions. It's not unlike a church meeting that goes way past the scheduled time. One person says, "Wow, the Holy Spirit was really moving," but you know the meeting was just poorly run. It doesn't honor God when we pretend to give him credit when we are actually blaming him for our poor decisions.

The Qoheleth tells us in Ecclesiastes that there is a season for everything, a time for every matter under heaven. That doesn't mean transitions won't be lonely and full of conflicting desires. Seasons of pastoral transition feel antithetical to pastoral ministry in the same way engagements are antithetical to marriages. Engagements are meant to end; marriages are not. Pastoral transition is about yanking up roots; pastoring involves putting roots down. Engagements are filled with frenetic activity and wedding-day planning; marriages thrive on the slow burn of love anchored in vows. Pastoral transition implies movement; pastoring requires standing with both feet in one neighborhood among one flock. Local churches are after all *lo-cal*—they have a place.

When I spoke with the elders of the church I was moving to about the uncomfortable way it affected my ministry at my current church, their reply was helpful. "Good," they said. "We wouldn't want to hire you at our church if you could leave a pastorate without being conflicted."

And they were right. Shepherds can, and perhaps should, let their eyes occasionally glance beyond their own flock, but those glances should be infrequent and primarily to look for straying sheep or predators, not to find a new flock altogether. Hired hands run when a wolf comes or when someone offers better pay. If you find yourself mourning the fact that you feel like a hired hand, that's a good sign. Hired hands rarely mourn transitions; they just move.

"Shepherd the flock of God that is among you," Peter writes in 1 Peter 5:2. I wish I could pull Peter aside and ask him what a pastor should do when transitioning from one flock to another flock, and—in a sense—there are potentially two flocks "among you." I think he'd tell us to embrace the tension we feel as a sign that we understand the gravity involved and, conversely, to consider it a warning sign if we can bail without angst.

I've spent the last few years studying pastoral transitions and interviewing dozens of pastors. The best piece of advice I received on the topic came in the line "Don't leave without feeling conflicted"—which, incidentally, was shared with me by the elders of the church I currently pastor. Seasons of pastoral transition are conflicting. They should be, so embrace the struggle.

9

THE GREATEST ENEMY OF THE CHURCH

It's Me, It's Me, O Lord, Standing in the Need of Prayer

These are times that try men's souls, but who is the enemy—the greatest enemy—of God's people?

Perhaps it's liberal Supreme Court judges and the sexual ethics of secular society. Or maybe it's ISIS and the looming threat of radical Islam. Perhaps it's the rapid increase of those that identify religiously as "none." Or maybe it's Planned Parenthood and others who advocate for an adult's right to comfort over a child's right to life and barbarically snuff out life in the very womb that is for its protection and growth.

As I look, from my limited vantage, around our world today, I don't know the answer to this question, at least, I don't know the answer exhaustively. But I do know the answer that the book of Judges gives, which is the same answer the whole Bible gives. According to Judges, if the people of God want to know who their greatest potential enemy is, they need only do one simple thing: Look in the mirror.

*   *   *

In the time of the judges, there were some scary-strong enemies. They oppressed, they pillaged, they raped as they saw fit
in their own eyes. And I'm sure if you did some man-on-the-
street interviews, you would have heard all sorts of external
reasons for their problems. "They have chariots and we don't,"
one Israelite might have said. "They are better fighters on the
plains than we are," says another. Or, "They have better gener-
als, better kings; that's why we're not inheriting the land."

Perhaps the *Jerusalem Post* of the day even ran headlines
telling this tale of woe. But if they did, it would have been superficial reporting. These were *not* the deepest issues. The
greatest enemies were not external, but internal. And the book
of Judges both shouts and whispers this indictment.

Consider the last sentence in the book. "Everyone did what
was right in his own eyes" (Judges 21:25; see also Judges 17:6).
This statement is the ancient equivalent of bold, italics, under-
line, and all caps, an example of the book shouting that the
greatest enemy is internal.

Another place is Judges 2:10, which is a key verse in the
book. Here the blame is laid on the fact that "there arose another generation . . . who did not know the LORD or the work
that he had done for Israel." Again, the foe is internal, not external.

But the book also whispers this message. For example, con-
sider the judge Tola (Judges 10:1–2). He, like another named
Shamgar, was a deliverer only mentioned in a verse or two
(Judges 3:31). But unlike Shamgar, who delivers from an external
enemy (the Philistines), no enemy is listed that Tola fought.
When Tola comes to save, he saves Israel from Israel.

And that is why the book, as a whole, concludes with an ap-
pendix of sordid stories likely from an earlier time in the book,
stories of a greedy priest, a Levite who dismembered his

concubine, and a civil war that nearly annihilated one of the tribes. Internal enemies, not external.

But it's not only Judges that makes this point, is it? Across covenants and authors—from Abraham, to David, to exile, to the church, to the second coming—the greatest issue is the purity and fidelity of our faith.

Peter speaks of Satan as our "enemy" and a "roaring lion" (1 Pet. 5:8), and Paul writes of our battle against "spiritual forces" (Eph. 6:12), but when Adam led us all into rebellion against God, his excuse that "the devil made me do it" didn't fly. Adam and Eve stopped delighting in God. Sure, there was an external enemy, but it was their faith, their inner life, that mattered most and led to their fall.

Consider when the twelve spies did their recon in Numbers 13–14. They felt like grasshoppers facing giants, but the issue was never their relative size, but rather, Would Israel trust the God of the grasshoppers?

And what about the end of Romans 1? After a notorious list of sins, the veritable punch in the gut is to the religious types, that is, those who should know better but apparently don't (Rom. 1:32).

And consider the letters to the churches in Revelation. The issue was not merely that someone, somewhere in the world was teaching something wrong, say, the "teaching of Balaam" or the "Nicolaitans." Rather, the issue was that some in the church "held" to this teaching (Rev. 2:14–15). And sure, in Thyatira "that woman Jezebel" was doing her thing, but God was on it ("I gave her time to repent . . . I will throw her onto a sickbed . . . I will strike her down," Rev. 2:20–24). The greatest threat to the church is whether they will "hold" to Jezebel's teaching or remain faithful to God's.

We could go on, but the point is clear: Not only Judges, but the whole of Scripture, teaches that the greatest enemy to God's people is internal.

And yet we deeply resist this teaching. Don't believe me? Does your church have a list of prayer requests? How many are related to spiritual apathy, fear of the Lord, love for the lost, divisions among brothers and sisters, and our subtle syncretism? How many prayer requests do we make to find our greatest joy in our Father's delight over us on account of the gospel? Not enough.

The greatest threat to the church is not ISIS or Planned Parenthood. It's not Hollywood. It's not atheist professors who ruin the faith of our sweet, Christian college freshmen. And the greatest enemies are not secular politicians and Supreme Court judges, or greedy corporations who hurt the poor and destroy the environment.

These challenges are real. The reality of babies killed, chopped, and sold as scrap metal is evil. And the Canaanite general Sisera, who "oppress[ed] the people of Israel cruelly" and raped captured women, was evil too (Judges 4:3; 5:28–30). However, it was when the people of God "abandoned the LORD and served the Baals and the Ashtaroth" (Judges 2:13), when their faith lost its purity and fidelity, and when internal (not external) idolatry became pandemic that the cookie crumbled.

If we want to know the worst enemy—the one that, apart from the sustaining grace of God, could eternally destroy us— then we must look in the mirror. Doing so won't be easy; it will be uncomfortable. But a long look into our own souls and indwelling sin might catch our melanoma while it's early. And if it does, praise God we have the gospel for our healing.

10

PASTOR, STRIVE TO LEARN THEIR NAMES

Another Way for Pastors to Shepherd Like Jesus

People say I'm naturally gifted at learning names. To some extent that might be true. The full truth, however, is I cheat.

But before I tell you *how* I cheat, let me stress *why*—as a pastor—I labor to learn the names of those who attend our church.

The reason we should learn names is twofold. First, a general reason: God has always existed in relationship, the loving relationship of Father, Son, and Spirit. And because we are made in God's image and likeness, it's not good for us to be alone. I believe this is the main reason why people desire to be where everyone knows their name, as in the tagline from the old show *Cheers*. God designed us for community.

There is also a specific reason why I want to excel at learning the names of my congregants. Embedded within the universal longing to be known, there seems to be echoes of the specific longing for relationship with God. We want our church shepherd to know the names of his sheep, just as the Good Shepherd knows the names of all his sheep (John 10:14).

Although many people in the Bible are nameless to us, God knows them. From the Israelites who were set free from Egypt, to the 7,000 who hadn't bowed the knee to Baal, to the 5,000 who ate the two fish and five loaves, to the 3,000 who were added to the church at Pentecost, to the countless multitude in Revelation—none is nameless to him. The Great Shepherd knows each by name.

And God's knowledge of his people is intimate, warm, and relational. Jesus knows his sheep's birthdays, their passions and longings, their wounds and fears, their sins and failures, the hairs on their heads and their length of days.

We'll never know all this about others, even all this about ourselves. Consequently, as pastors we must point people to Jesus as the Good Shepherd, not try to take his place. Nevertheless, Jesus's shepherding creates the paradigm for our shepherding. What Jesus does perfectly, we strive to approximate as we "shepherd the flock of God among [us]" (1 Pet. 5:2). And following this pattern means we must know the sheep he has put in our charge, starting with, and hopefully moving beyond, simply knowing their names.

Learning names is a skill we can improve with practice. I do several things to improve. With my last two ministry transitions, the process of learning names began during the interview stage. I'd scour the church's website and Facebook page looking for people in leadership. I also asked for access to their church picture directory (if they had one). Then, I'd make flash cards and study like I was cramming for a Hebrew exam. Perhaps this sounds excessive and a bit creepy, but it makes a huge difference. Once, when introduced to eight leaders in a group interview, they made the obligatory quip, "You probably won't remember our names." Yet over the next two hours I spoke to each person by name.

If this isn't for you, two more methods require less homework. First, when you end a conversation with someone new, ask, "Could you remind me of your name again?" This is socially acceptable because no one begrudges this the first time you meet, maybe even the second. It's often in restating the name that I catch it, especially if I repeat the name by saying something like, "I really enjoyed meeting you, Joe."

Also, ask people to restate their names each time they contribute during a Sunday school class or Bible study. People probably won't remember to do this, so you'll have to remind them a few times. If it's a lengthy meeting, however, don't make them continue doing it very long.

Be careful to make certain your effort to learn names doesn't seem insincere or conniving, as it's possible people will misunderstand your effort. Help them consider whether children feel slighted when their father makes the effort to thoughtfully prepare a surprise birthday party for them or whether a wife feels slighted when her husband works to prepare a surprise anniversary getaway. They probably won't. That's because sometimes it's the unseen effort, not merely the thought, that shows you really care.

Like most churches, mine has a transient fringe—those people who are neither members nor regular attendees. I'll never learn their names; indeed, they haven't given me a chance. And if this is true in my small church, it's that much more impossible for the lead pastor of a large church to know everyone's name. Still, we can make an effort to know more names than we do.

Learning names requires bravery; you have to be willing look foolish. As our church has grown in the last few years, it's been more difficult to keep names straight. Recently, I called one woman Jennifer, which wasn't her name, as she gently reminded me. Swing and a miss. But I've gotten her name right ever since.

Church members, you can help your pastors by going out of your way to remind them of your names and being patient when they get it wrong.

When you first begin attending a church, perhaps you could come early a few times or linger after a service to chat. It seems simple, but these things help local churches become a place where more of us know each other's names, which is a decent first step toward becoming the intimate community God desires. It's much more natural to "rejoice with those who rejoice" and "weep with those who weep" when the pastor knows your name is not Jennifer, but Jessica.

11

PASTORS NEED HEALTHY BOUNDARIES

The Sinful Folly of Burning Candles from Both Ends

There's a phrase in endurance sports called "burning matches." For every racer, there's an average pace that gets her to the finish line the fastest. And every time she increases her speed above this average pace, perhaps to catch one competitor or drop another, she "burns a match." This is part of racing, but the smart racer knows she has a finite number of matches to burn before her box is empty.

The same is true with pastoring. When you need to, you can sprint. The first hundred days in a new pastorate in a new church might be a good time to lift your pace, but you can't sprint the whole marathon. Slow and steady—with a few strategic bursts—is far more likely to win this often-grueling endurance race.

It's not as though we don't have boundaries and limitations anyway. There are only twenty-four hours in a day and only seven days in a week. Furthermore, you can only be in one place at a time. We can't go more than three days without water or a few dozen days without food.

God has given us boundaries and limitations. The *omni-*attributes (omnipresence, omnipotence, etc.) belong to God and God alone. Ministry isn't about one superhuman helping others become superhuman, but one human helping other humans to recover their true humanity by delighting and depending on Jesus.[1]

It's Satan who claims to offer a ministry without limitations: "You will be like God," he promises. "Just fall down and worship me, and you'll be so productive and famous you'll have all the kingdoms of the world and their glory."

But we won't be like God, at least not in these ways. As long as we exist, so will our limitations. Therefore, nightly sleep and weekly Sabbaths are declarations of faith that God is God and we are not. We are *his* creatures, and being his creatures is very good (Gen 1:31). Zack Eswine writes,

> You were never meant to repent because you can't fix everything. You were meant to repent because you've tried. Even if we could be god for people and fix it all, the fact remains that Jesus does not have the kind of fixing in mind that you and I want. . . . Sickness, death, poverty, and the sin that bores into and infests the human being will not be removed on the basis of any human effort, no matter how strong, godly, or wise that effort is.[2]

Therefore, pick a time to leave the office each day and stick to it. Years ago I got in the pattern of coming home around 4:30 p.m., and that's still what I do; it's when my family expects me. Also, establish your non-working days and stick to them, excluding the occasional wedding or funeral. Many pastors

---

[1] Definition of ministry adapted from Eswine, *The Imperfect Pastor*, 35.

[2] Ibid., 96–97.

choose either Monday or Friday as their day off, along with Saturday.

Additionally, set the number of nights a week you'll (typically) go back out for work. If your number is three or four, you can have a week where you're out six nights, but you can't do this week after week. If you need to keep track of the hours you've worked so they don't get out of hand, then do that. On the nights you are home, put your phone in another room. While you're at it, turn off all unnecessary notifications; it's hard to ignore a beeping, vibrating phone. You should also decide whether to give your cell number out, and if so, to whom.

When will you take appointments? Many pastors, including me, feel most productive when we schedule the mornings for study, preparation, and general admin while leaving meetings for the afternoon. This doesn't always work, but just as you watch your number of work nights, also watch how many meetings get scheduled outside of normal office hours.

It seems that it used to be more common for people to visit a pastor during the workday, much like we would expect to see a doctor. But this practice seems to be fading. Many of my appointments, if I let them, would gravitate toward times that are typically outside work hours, which means it's something I must watch closely.

Also, watch your eating. With so many evening meetings, it's easy to become unhealthy, as Gavin Ortlund points out:

> A pastor gets home from a difficult elder's meeting. It's
> nine o'clock in the evening, and it's been a long day. After
> a quick greeting to his wife, he beelines for the kitchen
> to reward himself from the burdens of the day by losing
> himself in Lay's potato chips, Red Vines licorice, and Dr.

Pepper. Several hours later, he turns off the television and heads to bed. The stress is gone.[3]

What's wrong with this? Nothing, every once in a while. And if you ask me, it's fine if the Dr. Pepper is an IPA. But if candy and carbonation binges become the norm, you're not healthy; you're probably medicating something below the surface.

Speaking of health, remember "physical training is of some value" (1 Tim 4:8 NIV). Among its benefits, many pastors find exercise to be a good boundary marker; it's a stone wall that keeps work hours from getting out of hand. In the past, when I've been injured and unable to exercise, I tend to overwork.

In no way am I suggesting my boundaries should be yours. You must establish your own healthy patterns. Just keep in mind that whatever boundaries you construct are there for your family, your fellow staff, your elders, and even your church members. It's hypocrisy to preach about our limits as humans and then to work as if these limits don't exist for you.

To run a good race, you'll have to occasionally pick up the pace, but when you do, just make sure you do so knowing you're burning matches. You don't want to be huffing and puffing for air before you've even crossed the first mile marker.

[3] Gavin Ortlund, "How to Fight Unhealthy Snacking: Dealing Well with Daily Depletion," *Desiring God*, July 7, 2015, http://www.desiringgod.org/articles/how-to-fight-unhealthy-snacking.

12

DO NOT DESPISE A GENTLE NUDGE

The Glory of Sanctification in the Seemingly Insignificant

A river cuts through Harrisburg, Pennsylvania where I live. Small rapids gurgle as the shallow water runs over rocks.

When my son and I have kayaked the river, we have learned—big surprise—that it's much harder to paddle *upstream* than *down*. But we have also learned that even when traveling downstream, you still have to paddle in order to steer. If you cannot steer, you drift along until you smack a boulder or get sucked into the counter-swirl of an eddy current. Avoiding these dangers sometimes requires paddling with all your might, but most often simply holding the tip of your paddle in the water at the proper angle is all that is necessary to avoid danger.

This idea is similar to how Christians understand obedience. There is a goodness to seeking mountain-top experiences with God when the chains of sin break and gospel joy erupts. Most of the time, however, walking with God entails small steps of obedience in the same direction over a long period of time. David Mathis calls these acts of devotion habits of grace. They often come from daily prayer, Bible reading, and weekly church attendance.

These little adjustments to our spiritual lives, while seemingly small and insignificant by themselves, make all the difference in avoiding spiritual danger and experiencing intimacy with God.

Nutritionists tell us that to lose one pound a week you must pull a calorie deficit of 3,500 calories a week, or about 500 calories a day. The path of weight loss might be more nuanced than this, but the points stands that losing weight requires not one massive 3,500-calorie decision, but a hundred smaller decisions. The same principle is true in dental hygiene. The dreaded dental pick is only there to scrape the plaque that gentle brushing can no longer clear. The ideal, however, is for a few minutes of brushing each day to have the desired effect.

Andy Crouch speaks to this in his book on technology. "An increasing body of psychological research suggests that our supply of willpower—the ability to make hard decisions that go against our instincts or preferences—is limited."[1] Crouch suggests, therefore, that we build "nudges" into our life that will help make our desired choices easier to make.

By *nudge* he does not mean *shove*. A nudge is a small force applied at the right time to a particular location in order to make a difference in the outcome. For example, making the clear-headed decision to only have a computer in public places will not stop you from looking at porn, but it can nudge you in the right direction. A shove would look more like taking a baseball bat to the motherboard.

My point is not to denigrate forceful action. The Bible speaks of God's word as heat that melts and a hammer that smashes (Jer. 23:29). The voice of the Lord can splinter

[1] Andy Crouch, *The Tech-Wise Family: Everyday Steps for Putting Technology in Its Proper Place* (Grand Rapids: Baker, 2017), 33.

individual cedar trees, shake the wilderness, and strip bark off an entire forest (Ps. 29). Sometimes this kind of force is necessary. Sometimes people do get caught in spiritual eddy currents, and soft paddling will not free them. They must paddle with all their might back into the stream of faithfulness. Jude speaks of saving certain sinners by "snatching them out of the fire" (1:23). That requires force.

But the Bible also portrays the word of God in softer imagery: as washing with a rag or as gentle rain falling on tender grass (Eph. 5:29; Deut. 32:2). As such, we should not despise the small and seemingly insignificant activities that keep us on the path of life. I believe this is what Paul means when he tells Timothy to keep a close watch on both his life and his doctrine so that he might save himself and those who sit under his teaching ministry (1 Tim. 4:16).

Most preachers get into a deadly theological pit not with a backhoe, but with a spoon, one little scoop at a time. Paul wants his son in the faith to make a habit of ladling grace into his life rather than sin because even small consistent scoops of grace will keep him away from danger. Quiet and unseen acts of piety may not have sound and fury, but they do signify something. As Tim Challies has observed, "We overestimate what God will do in us over a year but underestimate what God will accomplish in us through a lifetime."[2]

Examples of nudges in the Christian life abound. First, consider church discipline. Christians tend to think of church discipline only in the superlative—those rare and dramatic moments at an annual congregational meeting where somebody did something really bad, and now they're gonna get it.

[2] Tim Challies, "Maintaining Confidence in the Process," *Challies.com*, September 19, 2020, https://www.challies.com/articles/maintaining-confidence-in-the-process/.

This caricature of church discipline should be just that. When you put together Matthew 18:15–20, which teaches that as few people should be involved as possible, along with Galatians 6:1, which teaches that restoration should be done "in a spirit of gentleness," a very different picture of church discipline emerges. In a healthy church, discipline happens regularly among brothers and sisters who "bear one another's burdens, and so fulfill the law of Christ" (Gal. 6:2). Only when gentle nudges do not work should we apply more force.

Has God put someone in your life who needs a nudge?

Consider also how the confession of sin breathes life into our relationship with God. Recently, I confessed to our small group Bible study that I sensed bitterness creeping into my spiritual life. People had let me down, and I smoldered silently and sinfully about it.

On the one hand, confessing my bitterness to my small group and asking for prayer wasn't that big of a deal; I stood only ankle-deep in quicksand—no reason for serious alarm yet. But on the other hand, if I didn't confess, didn't ask for prayer, didn't repent to God, and didn't forgive those who hurt me, then before long I might have been neck-deep in bitterness. David reflects on what happened to him when he held back confession: "For when I kept silent, my bones wasted away" (Ps. 32:3).

Do you need to confess a sin to God and ask others to pray for you?

Finally, consider the way the imperfections in our local churches can work for a Christian's good. When local churches went online during Covid lockdowns, I kept hearing about church attendees who found a "better" church and preacher somewhere else online. Ordinarily our geographical bounded-ness kept us local, but the internet offers endless possibilities to find a better church, say, in Dallas or Denver even if we live in Decatur. And by "better," I mean a larger church with a more famous preacher and a snazzier online getup, as opposed to their less sexy church where a no-name pastor prays for his sheep by name.

Why, I wonder, was this trade so easy to make for some church attendees? Perhaps because the trade was a symptom rather than a cause. Perhaps the cause is that many wrongly understand Christianity and weekly gatherings as a series of self-help shoves toward self-actualization. If a big church with a better pastor can produce more umph, then just get your spiritual nuggets from that church instead.

But what if overlooking small imperfections in our weekly gatherings and serving God among imperfect saints is part of the very plan God has chosen to develop us into spiritual maturity and stir our affections for that which only he can satisfy?

In the last year, have you been tempted to think meanly of your local church and its pastors?

In his classic A *Long Obedience in the Same Direction*, the late Eugene Peterson wrote, "There is a great market for religious experience in our world; there is little enthusiasm for the patient acquisition of virtue, little inclination to sign up for a long apprenticeship in what earlier generations of Christians called holiness."[3] Here, and throughout his life of faithfully pastoring small churches, Peterson critiques our lust for epic experiences while showing the beauty and power of piety in the seemingly mundane, the small nudges that apprentice us toward holiness.

[3] Eugene Peterson, A *Long Obedience in the Same Direction*, 20th Anniversary Edition (Downers Grove, IL: InterVarsity, 2003), 16.

When we read our Bibles each day and no angels dance on the page, when we pray and the walls of a prison do not shake, and when we speak and revival does not break out, that's okay, because when obedience happens, however seemingly small and unnoticeable, nothing never happens. Keeping the rudder of a ship pointed away from danger might not feel all that significant but tiny course corrections would have kept the Titanic from missing the iceberg, just as nudges keep us walking intimately with God.

13

DON'T LET SEXUAL SHAME MOVE YOU FROM CHRIST'S MISSION

How the Gospel Provides Hope for Ministers Too

Pastor and author John Piper has said the closest he ever came to being fired from his long tenure as pastor of Bethlehem Baptist Church was when he wrote an article entitled "Missions and Masturbation."[1]

Provocative title, huh? He writes,

One of the major forces preventing young people from obeying the call of God into vocational Christian service is defeat in the area of lust. A teenager hears a challenging call to throw himself into the cause of world evangelization. He feels the promptings of the Holy Spirit. He tastes the thrill of following the King of kings into battle. But he does not obey because he is

[1] John Piper, "Missions and Masturbation," *Desiring God*, September 10, 1984, http://www.desiringgod.org/articles/missions-and-masturbation.

masturbating regularly. He feels guilty . . . So he feels un-
worthy and unable to obey the call of God.[2]

Reflecting on the article from years later, Piper noted his
words were birthed out of the sadness he felt over so many
people, young people especially, "lost in the cause of Christ's
mission because they were not taught how to deal with the guilt
of sexual failure."[3]

Note carefully what he did *not* say. He didn't say that many
people were lost to the mission of Christ *because of sexual failure.* Piper's point is more specific. He argued that many were
lost to the mission of Christ because they didn't know how to
deal with the guilt and shame that come from sexual failure.
They messed up and moved on with life, and in the process, also
moved on from missions because they didn't know how to deal
with their guilt. What a sad outcome.

Piper published the original article in September of 1984,
which is over thirty-five years ago! But I suspect Piper's concern is still relevant. Sexual sin and its associated guilt and
shame are just as prevalent today, if not more so.

While guilt and shame over sin are typically understood as
negative, I want to start by saying they can actually be signs of
spiritual health. After many centuries consumed with sin, the
indictment God levels against his people is that they no longer
know how to blush (Jer. 6:15). Their sinful patterns killed their
ability to even know what is shameful. Adam and Eve shouldn't
have taken the fruit or hidden from God, but at least they knew
enough to know they did something wrong.

---

[2] Ibid.

[3] John Piper, "How to Deal with the Guilt of Sexual Failure for the Glory of Christ
and His Global Cause," *Desiring God*, January 4, 2007, http://www
.desiringgod.org/messages/how-to-deal-with-the-guilt-of-sexual-failure-for-
the-glory-of-christ-and-his-global-cause.

But I should also point out that no matter how much shame we feel, no amount of shame over sin can atone for our sin. We can't blush enough to buy forgiveness. In his book about the struggle with pornography, John Cusick writes that in penance "a man takes the shame he carries and attempts to overcome it somehow through performance. It's an unconscious way of atoning for our sin, because deep down we believe our struggle makes us less acceptable to God."[4] Cusick isn't advocating for penance to deal with our sin; he's just describing a common solution, a solution that really is no solution at all.

We often associate penance with Roman Catholicism, but as Protestants we have our own forms of penance. Do you ever find yourself in a flurry of good deeds to show God how sorry you are? I know a man who would randomly do hours and hours of hard labor on church construction projects. In hindsight, we learned the tornado of saw dust was his attempt to deal with his shame over his sexual sin. Or perhaps you find yourself pouting to show God how much you want to be forgiven. We can mope about our house or church, but by itself, presenting our sadness to God atones for zero sins (Heb. 9:22).

Stand back from these questions and consider the bigger picture. Why do you think working off our sins or wallowing in them are such common experiences? Could it be that these are the default "gospels" of our hearts? I think so. We try to work off our sexual sin to earn God's love. And we lament our sin because our sadness shows God—so we think—how much we know we don't deserve his love, which is a convoluted way to show God we do deserve his love. Paul would call the whole thing—working off sin or wallowing over sin—"a different gospel" (Gal. 1:7, 8). And different gospels don't save. Only the real one does.

---

[4] Michael John Cusick, *Surfing for God: Discovering the Divine Desire Beneath Sexual Struggle* (Nashville: Thomas Nelson, 2012), 92.

To John Piper's point above, too many people are lost to the mission of Christ because they don't know the solution to sexual sin is the same solution to all sin. As Christians, we need repentance, *not* penance. We need faith, *not* performance. There's an eternal difference. Salvation is found only through the love of Jesus for us. And once we're saved through him and by him, we're free. Simply free (Gal. 5:1).

If you're currently leading a ministry and your sexual sin is to such an extent that it disqualifies you, then you need to step down. It's important that you get your sexual struggles under control before you worry about ministering to others. John Piper's concern for people bailing on the mission of Christ shouldn't be taken to mean that a person should continue headstrong in public ministry regardless of the extent of sexual sin. That's not the point. The point is that whatever you do for a living—whether you continue in vocational ministry or now work a construction job—no matter our struggle with sexual sin, don't stop serving Jesus.

If you need time away from public ministry, the outworking of your Christian ministry may look different and be less visible—indeed, it should be less visible—but keep fighting; keep struggling against sexual sin and helping others do the same. "Let us not grow weary of doing good," Paul wrote, "for in due season we will reap, if we do not give up" (Gal. 6:9). Paul warns against weariness because the temptation to quit is real.

But maybe as you read this, you don't need to step away from ministry because years and years ago you already did, and you don't feel worthy to begin again. Stop. You'll never feel worthy because you won't ever be worthy. No one will. I'd encourage you to seek out a friend, pastor, or missionary who could help you discern if it might be right to re-engage in missions.

"The tragedy," Piper says, "is that Satan uses the guilt of

[sexual sin] to strip you of every radical dream you ever had, or might have . . ." Piper continues by saying that in the place of your dreams for world evangelization, Satan gives "you a happy, safe, secure, American life of superficial pleasures until you die in your lakeside rocking chair, wrinkled and useless, leaving a big fat inheritance to your middle-aged children to confirm them in their worldliness. That's the main tragedy." [5]

That paragraph might be just as provocative as an article titled "Missions and Masturbation." But I think he's right. Friend, the gospel you so long to share with others is not simply good news for them. It's good news for you too. Give Christ your sin and your shame. He wants them both.

[5] Piper, "How to Deal with the Guilt of Sexual Failure for the Glory of Christ and His Global Cause."

14

THE TRUTH IS ALWAYS POSITIVE

A Tale of Two Books

I had only been a pastor at our church for a month or two, and so far I hadn't preached anything too controversial. As a new teaching pastor, I thought it best to lay down some solid sermons before saying anything spicy; the congregation and I were just getting to know each other.

But then we began a series in the book of Proverbs, and I was assigned the sermon on sex.

That Sunday morning got off to a bumpy start. When I arrived at church, I awkwardly went over the Scripture slides with the young woman volunteering to run the computer, passages from chapters 5–7 of Proverbs about "breasts" and "intoxication." The clicker looked like she was ten years old because she was. As if I wasn't already feeling uncomfortable, as the music team began the first song, my new neighbor walked in the back of the church and came to the front row. I had shared the gospel with him the other day, and he came to church with his girlfriend. They lived together and now had a literal front row seat to a sermon on sex their first for time in our church.

A few days later, as we debriefed the sermon, our other teaching pastor told me I preached nothing wrong—it was, in a sense, all true. The problem, he said, was my timidity about the truth, even an embarrassment that conveyed to the congregation that while God's word might be true, it's not actually good for us.

In the spring of 2020 two books from two major publishers released the same week, with each author covering similar ground but from different convictions. The topic of the books, broadly speaking, is anthropology: who we are as humans and why understanding our humanity matters. One author took a biblical view and the other, by and large, did not. Both books still seem to be selling well.

The first book is Brant Hansen's *The Truth About Us: The Very Good News about How Very Bad We Are.*[1] The second book is Mike McHargue's *You're a Miracle (and a Pain in the Ass): Embracing the Emotions, Habits, and Mystery That Make You You.*[2] The authors share a lot in common, including being known for their winsome, humorous speaking platforms, whether by radio or podcast. The books also share a lot of common ground. But as the subtitles suggest, the two roads diverge. Hansen's book understands the gospel of Jesus as the good news to our badness; McHargue sees our acceptance of ourselves (and others) as the good news. Here's a closer look at each of their arguments.

*   *   *

[1] Brant Hansen, *The Truth About Us: The Very Good News about How Very Bad We Are* (Grand Rapids: Baker, 2020).

[2] Mike McHargue, *You're a Miracle (and a Pain in the Ass): Embracing the Emotions, Habits, and Mystery That Make You You* (New York: Convergent Books, 2020).

Hansen opens *The Truth About Us* with a "Dear Everyone" letter that simply says, "We all have a serious problem: All of us think we're good people. But Jesus says we're not. Sincerely, Brant P. Hansen / PS: The rest of the book is the PS."

And the rest of the book is that postscript, two hundred pages exploring what Jesus says about our depravity and the Savior's love for real sinners, not theoretical ones. In classic Hansen style, self-deprecating stories abound. But he also treads serious terrain. "Repentance is rare and revolutionary and arduous and counter to our every instinct," he writes, because it requires "reversing all the psychological machinery" that wants to blame others. He then adds, "But if we don't repent, we never get to feel the pure joy of forgiveness." [3] In other words, walking through the door of truth requires the humility to acknowledge our badness, but this is the only way we come to know God, the meaning of the cross, and our heavenly adoption.

McHargue fills his book *You're a Miracle (and a Pain in the Ass)* with fascinating scientific discussion, especially about how the human brain operates. But the book is more than facts and figures. McHargue is a gifted storyteller who pulls readers in with his engaging and transparent prose, even telling us of his attempted suicide as a teenager. Throughout *You're a Miracle*, as with his first book *Finding God in the Waves*, McHargue refuses to adopt the tone of an angry ex-evangelical, someone too jaded to appreciate aspects of the tradition he now rejects. I commend him for that.

We can begin to see the difference between Hansen's good news and McHargue's in this extended quote in the first chapter of *You're a Miracle*:

---

[3] Hansen, *The Truth about Us*, 126.

If I plumb the depths of what science reveals about my mind and body, it can lead me to a place of remarkable peace with myself. . . . This is a book about you learning that you are a miracle too. I want to start you on a journey that ends with you looking in the mirror one day, unable to hold back tears, because instead of seeing someone who isn't tall, thin, young, or attractive enough, you instead see a profound and rare being *who is worthy of love*. I want you to see yourself and be awed, because you are truly awesome.[4]

An evangelical Christian could affirm much of this quote. God pronounced his creation "good," and the heavens declare his glory, and yet it was only after God made male and female in his image that God called creation "very good." Thus humans are, in McHargue's words, indeed a miracle.

Yet McHargue's emphasis on human worthiness encapsulates the difference between the two books, a difference as significant as the difference between Christianity and Christendom. The former possesses the true gospel of acceptance by God through the work of Christ, while the latter leaves orthodoxy for the gospel of self-acceptance. It is not surprising that McHargue says near the end of the book, "I am a Christian. But I am the kind whom most American Christians wouldn't call a Christian."[5]

Our hearts want a gospel of self-acceptance, and we'll buy books that tell us so. But as Jesus told the Pharisees, he came not to call those who saw themselves as healthy and righteous but those who knew their sin and sickness (Mark 2:17).

---

[4] McHargue, *You're a Miracle*, 18, emphasis added.
[5] Ibid., 177.

Progressive Christianity would love to identify evangelicals with the Pharisees in the Bible because of our supposed fastidious attention to jots and tittles, but—at least in this way of calling the sick healthy—it is progressive Christianity that shares the family likeness. J. Gresham Machen noted one hundred years ago, "Without the conviction of sin there can be no appreciation of the uniqueness of Jesus . . . . [and] without the conviction of sin, the good news of redemption seems to be an idle tale."[6] The real gospel allows us to stand in front of the mirror unable to hold back tears, because instead of seeing someone who isn't tall, thin, young, or attractive enough, we know God's love has drowned all our unworthiness in an endless ocean of grace.

We talk of parents having teachable moments with their children; that one Sunday years ago when I preached about sex from the book of Proverbs as a new pastor to a new congregation taught me more in one sermon than a year of preaching. We happened to have a church picnic that afternoon, and I confessed to an older, seasoned Christian some of the reasons why I felt so timid about the truth. He looked at me and said something I've not forgotten: "Just remember, the truth is always positive."

In a day when the truth that sinners need a Savior can feel antiquated, as though biblical anthropology were an aspect of the once-for-all-delivered gospel to leave behind, Christians might need to double-down on the bad news to appreciate the good.

---

[6] J. Gresham Machen, *Christianity & Liberalism* (Grand Rapids: Eerdmans, 1997 edition, original 1923), 105–6.

15

LIGHT FOR THOSE WHO SIT IN DARKNESS

What Christmas Says About Our Sin

Christians around the world are celebrating Christmas this week and preparing our hearts and minds to behold the beauty of Jesus.

Sometimes, however, the celebrations in our hearts are less enthusiastic than all the lights and songs around us. Our hearts do not always explode with fireworks at the joy of the incarnation. Instead, they often flicker like the feeble rays of a single votive candle.

One reason we lack passion for Christmas is that we often fail to truly see God as holy, and our sin as serious. Therefore, we do not have as much joy in Christ's coming as we could.

I've been reading a series of novels by Marilynne Robinson, which includes *Gilead*, *Home*, and *Lila* (and now *Jack*). Each novel tells a version of the same story through the eyes of a different character. The stories center around two pastors and their families in the small town of Gilead, Iowa, around the middle of the last century. The second book, *Home*, tells the story from the perspective of Glory, the daughter of the Presbyterian minister Robert Boughton.

In the novel, Glory describes the spiritual complacency of her town and of her father's preaching about sin.

> Complacency was consistent with the customs and manners of Presbyterian Gilead and was therefore assumed to be justified in every case. . . . Even her father's sermons treated salvation as a thing for which they could be grateful as a body. . . . He did mention sin, but it was rarefied in his understanding of it, a matter of acts and omissions so commonplace that *no one could be wholly innocent of them or especially alarmed by them,* either—the uncharitable thought, the neglected courtesy . . .[1]

What kind of sins might have been discussed in these sermons? Apparently, nothing too disturbing. According to Glory, her father was preaching about the sins like failing to call your mother on her birthday, or judging the homeless man on the side of the road, or not returning emails fast enough, or not helping the neighbor kid with her fundraiser.

It seems Reverend Boughton preached about transgressions so innocent and un-alarming as to hardly require salvation at all. We've all made mistakes, dropped the ball, and fallen short. These kinds of sins happen, and we're sorry about it, but we're not necessarily alarmed by them. Don't misunderstand me, though. My negative comments about Reverend Boughton's preaching are not a reflection of my view of the novel or the series, which I'm thoroughly enjoying. Likewise, please do not think I advocate, instead, error in the opposite direction.

[1] Marilynne Robinson, *Home* (New York: Picador, 2009), 111, emphasis added.

My point is simply that Boughton's light-on-sin-preaching, wherever it does exist, is a shame. It's a shame *not* because it's wimpy preaching ("real preachers preach about sin"). Rather, this type of preaching is unbecoming to ministers because it's not faithful to the Bible, which is the true measure of Christian preaching—not our personal preferences. In the Bible, sin is certainly an ugly, fearsome, insidious thing, which wars against God and against anyone who believes its lies. Consider what Jesus says in Mark 7:21–23:

> For from within, out of the heart of man, come evil thoughts, sexual immorality, theft, murder, adultery, coveting, wickedness, deceit, sensuality, envy, slander, pride, foolishness. All these evil things come from within, and they defile a person.

In short, sin *is* alarming.

But why is sin alarming? It's not because the sins Jesus mentions above are "bad" and other sins are "less bad." All sin is alarming, because all sin is against a holy God. Even the sins some consider petty, or as Glory puts it, "commonplace," are serious, because they are committed against an infinitely holy and just God.

And if sin against a holy God is serious, then we should despair. Christians, however, need not despair. We need not despair because there is a Savior who took our place, becoming our sin and bearing the full weight of our punishment (Mark 14:36; Rom. 3:25–26). It's this good news that causes the apostle Paul to burst into song in 1 Corinthians 15:55. Because of the incarnation, life, death, and resurrection of Jesus, he writes, "O death, where is your victory? O death, where is your sting?"

The awesome joy of salvation is anchored in the awful seriousness of sin. This theme frequently occurs in our beloved Christmas hymns. Take, for example, the familiar lines in "O

Holy Night." Yes, "long lay the world in sin and error pining," but this is not the whole story. The verse continues, "the weary world rejoices" when the Savior appears.

It's the times when I have seen my sin as deeply offensive to God—not as minor mistakes or foibles or idiosyncrasies of my personality—that the story of Jesus has actually been truly good news, and not a cliché. This kind of self-reflection requires courage. Timothy Keller writes,

> Are you willing to say, "I am a moral failure. I don't love God with all my heart, soul, strength, and mind. I don't love my neighbor as myself. And, therefore, I am guilty, and I need forgiveness and pardon"? It takes enormous courage to admit these things, because it means throwing your old self-image out and getting a new one through Jesus Christ. And yet that is the foundation for all the other things that Jesus can bring into your life— all the comfort, all the hope, all the joyful humility, and everything else.[2]

This Christmas may God cause our hearts to explode with real joy over the salvation that comes through Jesus. If that is going to happen, we first need the courage to reckon seriously with the darkness within us. And if we do this, then we'll truly appreciate that "a light has dawned" among us (Matt. 4:16).

---

[2] Timothy Keller, *Hidden Christmas: The Surprising Truth Behind the Birth of Christ* (New York: Viking, 2016), 60–61.

16

TWO WAYS EVERY CHRISTIAN
CAN BE PASTORAL

Shepherding a Church Requires Each Part Working Properly

The last time I saw my grandfather alive he made fun of me for being a pastor. You've probably heard the jokes or even made them yourself. "What does a pastor do all week anyway? You only work like one hour."

That's one extreme view, the view of a pastor who works little. The other extreme is a pastor who works all the time, like eighty hours a week, and no one else in the congregation does anything because "real ministry" only counts as such when done by professionals. Yet there is no way most churches, my own church included, could exist if only a handful of pastors did all the pastoring.

You may have heard the phrase, "A man's home is his castle." The saying, as I understand it, maintains that no matter the actual wealth of the owner, size of the home, or lineage to nobility, there is a dignity to the owner and his home. The home may not be a castle, but he's still the king of the castle.

As Christians, we could tweak the phrase to something like, "A Christian's church is their parish." Of course, the word parish reminds us of priests and Roman Catholicism, but don't get hung up on that. I simply mean to say every Christian has the responsibility and privilege of being pastoral. God speaks of his people this way in both the Old and New Testaments. When God saved his people from the house of slavery in Egypt, he told them they would be "a kingdom of priests" (Ex. 19:6). Later, God set apart the specific tribe of Levi for the task of full-time, vocational ministry. But the principle was clear: whether you're a Levite or not, the whole nation of Israel was to be priestly. In the New Testament, the Apostle Peter picks up on this same language when he speaks of all Christians as "a royal priesthood" called to "proclaim the excellencies" of God (1 Pet. 2:9). We most often associate proclaiming with preachers, but Peter encourages us that, though only some proclaim from a pulpit, every Christian preaches.

You don't need the office of pastor to be pastoral. In fact, your church would shrivel and die if the Christians within your church stopped pastoring. There's way too much pastoring to go around for only the pastors to pastor.

Think about it like this. Doctors are great, but the medical community would become crippled if every kid who scraped his knee had to go to the ER.

Yet, just as with medical procedures, there are some things better left to those called to the office of pastor, as spoken of in passages such as 1 Timothy 3:1–7. In all things, Scripture should be our guide. But as I think about the church I pastor, many ways come to mind that we could grow in "church-wide pastoral ministry," but I wish we engaged two particular areas with more passion.

First, every Christian can pastor by seeking sheep who stray. It doesn't take a large church for people to fall through the cracks, though "falling through the cracks" has become a cliché that makes us callous to the reality. The actual experience can leave bruises that don't heal quickly. An older woman and long-time attender at our church went to the hospital for several days, underwent a surgery, and came home. No one from our church called or even noticed. So she and her husband left our church. I noticed, called, and apologized weeks later when I found out what happened. I wish she had stayed; it's both the pastor's responsibility to know their sheep and also the sheep's responsibility to call their shepherds when they are sick (James 5:14). Regardless, I contend she'll recover faster from her surgery than being ignored by her church. Falling through the cracks hurts.

Christians have always found encouragement that Jesus is the kind of shepherd who leaves the ninety-nine secure sheep to find the one lost sheep (Luke 15:1–7), which is why pastoral ministry must involve this same emphasis, seeking those on the fringes and pulling them back. When you notice a person miss a few weeks in a row, find ways to follow up. Sometimes it's actually easier for the Christian in a pew to notice a person missing in action than a pastor who is up front. And don't fear you'll be prying into people's business. I know if I left a church, I'd want people to notice. Wouldn't you?

Second, every Christian can pastor by discipling others. I know that discipling, not unlike preaching, can sound like the sort of thing only done by professional Christians. But it's not. A disciple just means a follower of Jesus, and part of being a follower of Jesus involves helping others follow him. It's what we do. As a pastor, discipling is a part of my job, yet our church would be far more healthy if dozens of people were doing it too.

You might not feel ready or equipped to seek out someone to disciple on your own. I'd recommend you approach a pastor in your church and tell him you wanted to disciple others. I'm sure he would help you.

Here's one more way to pastor through discipleship. If you come to church with people, before the conversation slides to what's for lunch, who's mowing the lawn, and how much you're ready for a nap, keep the conversation on the worship service— what confused, challenged, convicted, and comforted you.

I'm sure people at my church talk about my sermons on the way home when I preach a lousy or controversial one, but I wish the pastoral debriefing of the ways God spoke through his word to our hearts became the norm.

The membership book I wrote for our church is called *Each Part Working Properly*. The title comes from a phrase in Ephesians 4:16 where Paul writes that when each part of the body of Christ works properly, the body "builds itself up in love."

I often think of this as a beautiful reversal of the game of Jenga. When you play Jenga, as the wooden structure gets taller, the whole thing becomes less stable. But that's not the way Paul says it should be in local churches. When each part engages in pastoral ministry, the church gets more stable, not less.

My grandpa never really attended church, hence his confusion about my role as a pastor and how much I work. But I wish he had attended, not only so he could have heard me preach the gospel but also so he could have experienced the love of Jesus Christ embodied by a church full of pastors.

17

ON PASTORAL PRAYER

It Should Not Be So Difficult for Me, but It Is

In the summer of 2019 the pastor-elders of our church listened to a 9Marks podcast about leading corporate prayers during church worship services.[1] We found Jonathan Leeman and Mark Dever's discussion both stimulating and convicting. We even made the change to incorporate more time for meaningful prayer during our worship services.

Now, each of our pastor-elders takes a Sunday to pray before the offering is collected, which is typically done right before the sermon. Sometimes teaching and travel schedules are such that an elder-qualified man who is not currently a pastor-elder may lead the prayer. But you get the idea. The prayer typically lasts around five minutes and often has overlap with the themes of the morning sermon. I'm so thankful Scott, one of our lay pastor-elders, initiated and maintains this ministry.

One weekend in January of 2020 when I wasn't preaching, it was my turn to lead the pastoral prayer. We had a worship

[1] Jonathan Leeman and Mark Dever, "Pastor's Talk, Episode 16: On Corporate Prayer," *9Marks*, May 30, 2017, https://www.9marks.org/pastors-talk/episode16/.

service that was less full than normal, so I took the opportunity to stretch us a bit by praying closer to ten minutes—well, maybe closer to fifteen. The length of the prayer stretched me too. And because we've recently had an influx of newcomers, I used the opportunity to pray through our church's five-year goals that were current at the time. Our leaders think and pray about these often, but, admittedly, we do a poorer job of keeping them in front of our people.

Jesus warned against praying in public to be seen by others (Matt. 6:1–4). But Jesus did not mean this as an indictment against all public prayer, for he immediately proceeded to teach us what we call the Lord's Prayer. In the hope that my prayer flows out of the stream of healthy public prayer, not the stream of sinful public prayer, I share my pastoral prayer from that Sunday morning in the hope that it will encourage others to make public pastoral prayer an increasingly important part of local church services.

*   *   *

Heavenly Father, we pause when looking over our goals. We do not want to be like those described in the book of James, those who in their arrogance and self-reliance presumed that by simply putting in time and effort they could bring about their goals of more profit and more abundance, not realizing their lives—indeed, *our* lives—depend upon you for strength and energy. Our hearts do not beat, and our lungs do not breathe, apart from your sustaining grace. We read in the book of Hebrews that your Son upholds the universe by the word of his power. The planets of the solar system continue to orbit because you say so, just as the details of our lives are held in place because you say so.

Yet, Lord—acknowledging your sovereignty, acknowledging your goodness, acknowledging the power of the gospel that is at work among us—we come boldly before your throne of grace for help in our time of need.

Plant a Church

Heavenly Father, we ask that you would help us plant another church in the city of Harrisburg, not for our glory and fame but for the name and renown of the one who spilled his blood so that more and more people could taste and see the goodness of the Lord.

We thank you for those who, some twenty years ago, left the comfort of a great church so they might, by your grace and power, labor to see our church built up in love. May you even now be giving some among us that same kind of pioneering, sacrificial spirit who see the name of Jesus being magnified as of more importance than the comfort of attending an established church.

Pursue a "New" Facility & Care for our Local Community

Heavenly Father, when we began to look for a new church building, we had no idea how difficult it would be. I had no idea how difficult it would be. At first, all the options, few as they were, seemed bad. And, so, we give you praise for our church building. We thank you for the beauty of the renovations you enabled us to complete eighteen months ago and the way people continue to come to this church building and find hope and peace and comfort. Lord, we thank you for the neighborhood in which you placed us. We thank you for the gospel inroads that have been made into this community. May you enable us to become servants who seek to bless our neighbors in your name.

As we see brokenness around us—whether it be the search for joy that takes place in the strip clubs just around the corner or the quiet lives of desperation led by many who feel alone in their homes—we pray that you would make our church building a safe place, a place where people can heal and find joy that will truly satisfy.

Increase Racial and Ethnic Diversity

Heavenly Father, please help our church to grow in racial and ethnic diversity as a testimony to the uniting power of the gospel. We thank you for those among us who enrich our lives by bringing other perspectives. We thank you for the dozens of people who come to our building three days a week to learn English. We thank you especially for those who have taken a particular interest in the immigrants and refugees among us. Lord, please forgive us for being slower to help than we ought; forgive us for being reluctant to reach out; forgive us for being hesitant to love.

Forgive us, Lord, for using the pronouns *us* and *them*.

Stay Streamlined, Program-Light

Heavenly Father, when we set the goal to be streamlined and program-light at our church, we did not intend to stifle the work of your Holy Spirit among us. Forgive us, Lord, if that has happened or is currently happening. Lord, we do not want to be streamlined and program-light because it's easier or because it allows us to remain lazy, preferring *our* comfort over *your* mission. We do not aim to be streamlined and program-light so we can have more Netflix.

Instead, we believe we should measure spiritual maturity not by how often we attend church meetings other than Sunday mornings but by how many of our neighbors and co-workers we know well enough and have loved well enough that they could ask us to pray for them when their lives seem to be crashing down around them.

In a culture that applies increasing pressure to do more and more and more, we ask that you help us to intentionally build margin into our lives so that when the Spirit does lead us to begin new ministries, we can participate in them with joy and obedience. Lord, we long to stay streamlined and program-light so that the members of this church are not so burdened with the ministry initiatives of our leaders that they can't be free to serve you wholeheartedly as your Spirit leads them; we long for a passion for new ministries to bubble up from within the hearts of those who call this church home. Lord, I thank you for the new ministry of the Christmas Giving Tree that will bless those among us with Christmas presents signifying, in tangible ways, your love for us. We've never done this before, but I thank you, Lord, for placing the idea upon the hearts of a few individuals and giving them the vision and obedience to see it become a reality.

Expand Evangelism Ministry

Heavenly Father, we pray for our evangelism ministry. Oh, that you would cause your gospel to go forth from us with greater power. Lord, as we share the story of the life, death, resurrection, and second coming of the Son of God, oh that more and more people would come to understand the sacrifice you made for them. Lord, would you cause your good news to be received by us in such a way that it is actually treasured as good news, news we long to share with others. Forgive us that our love for you is so small that we find it easier to talk about news here today and gone tomorrow.

Connect and Disciple Newcomers

Heavenly Father, you commanded us to go and make disciples of all nations, to baptize people into the name of the Father, the Son, and the Holy Spirit. You promised that your authority, your power, and your presence will be with us as we do so. I pray for the many relationships that have formed among our church, relationships not built around simply having coffee or watching our children play together, but relationships intentionally seeking to help one another be conformed to the image of Jesus Christ.

Lord, many at our church have no idea what being in a discipleship relationship would be like—to have someone to offer sound, biblical counsel into their lives and to have someone to weep with when their children walk away from the faith. Lord, would you make us into the type of church where discipleship relationships are not only natural but normal, that we would be the type of church where it would be seen as rare and unusual to *not* be in intentional discipleship relationships.

I pray especially for the older, mature Christians among us who were never themselves discipled by someone else. I pray that though they never received such care, they would build into others, giving what they never directly received.

As I think about the connection's ministry of our church, Lord, I pray for the new pastor we are seeking to hire. We've been looking and praying for the last six months and are currently interviewing pastors. Give us wisdom; we need it.

Lord, I think about what one candidate said when we asked what it might look like for a connections ministry to thrive here at Community. He said it might look not so much like one new pastor doing all the work of connections but rather like a congregation who sees themselves more and more as the connection pastors and like a church where a young couple notices an elderly couple who needs care and love and, unprompted by staff pastors, the young and the old couple move toward each other in love. Lord, yes, for more and more of this kind of connection here among us.

Increasingly Become a Church of Prayer

Finally, Heavenly Father, we ask you to make us a church that increasingly values prayer. I don't think we are good at this; I know I am not good at this. Praying to you in a church service for ten uninterrupted minutes should not be as difficult as it is. Forgive me for thinking I can build your church simply through effort and time on task. Forgive me for mistaking commotion and activity and sawdust flying around in the air for the substance of true spiritual life. Lord, we will cast our cares upon you when we see the weakness of our shoulders and the futility of our ingenuity.

As we call out to you in prayer—as a church gathered together in unity on Sunday mornings; as a church scattered around the city in small group Bible studies during the week; as families and homes and individuals who follow you when no one is watching but you—Lord, surprise us with the beauty of your grace, the joy of your forgiveness, and the peace of your presence.

So we ask all this, Heavenly Father, knowing you can do more than we could ask or imagine. And we pray all this in the name of Jesus Christ, by which we mean our prayers are prayed consistent with Christ's will (not our will), and our prayers are prayed upon Christ's authority (not our authority).

Amen.

18

THE WRATH OF GOD SHOULD COME TO OUR MINDS MORE OFTEN

What We Miss When We Miss Out on God's Wrath

A.W. Tozer famously said that "what comes into our minds when we think about God is the most important thing about us."[1]

I doubt many modern Christians think first of God's wrath when they think about him. There have been times in redemptive history, though, when God's wrath would have sat heavily upon the minds of God's people, such as on the afternoon Uzzah touched the ark or when John saw visions on the island of Patmos.

Today, however, the image in Revelation of a rider on a white horse tromping through the red froth of the winepress of the wrath of the Almighty does not come into our minds often.

And I'm not sure it should; the Bible says, "God is love," not "God is wrath" (1 John 4:1).

---

[1] A.W. Tozer, *Knowledge of the Holy: The Attributes of God* (New York: Harper Collins, org. 1961), 1.

At our church, we have not had a topical sermon on God's wrath, nor on any of God's attributes, in the last half dozen years. Maybe we should. We typically leave pointed discussions like this to our adult Sunday School classes. But the other week, in a sermon talking about the fear of man and the fear of God, I preached from Matthew 10 where Jesus told his disciples, "And do not fear those who kill the body but cannot kill the soul. Rather fear him who can destroy both soul and body in hell" (v. 28).

Rather than pushing past these words quickly, I encouraged us to linger. I told our people to notice that it's not necessarily either the hotness of hell or the lasting nature of hell that Jesus says to fear. Hell is hot and hell is long, I said, but that's not what we should fear. Jesus essentially says, "Don't fear people most; don't fear hell most; fear the God who can toss you into hell." I told our people that this short verse should cause us to tremble.

My hope in lingering over these heavy realities was not to preach for gratuitous shock and awe. Neither was my hope to stir unmitigated fear. Just two verses later, Jesus tells his disciples to "fear not" because he cares for those disciples, just as he cares for us.

I said what I said because it's true, and also because the truth of God's wrath—when rightly understood by the Christian—is good for us. Each week I preach to people weary and heavy-laden by sin, sometimes by the sin of others, sometimes by their own, and sometimes both. We may not need a sermon on God's wrath each Sunday, but we are impoverished, even malnourished, in three particular ways if the burning fury of God's wrath never comes into our minds.

*   *   *

When we forget God's wrath, we have to display our own wrath. We are quick to decry the wrongs of others, especially on social media. But could our hair-trigger for injustice go deeper than our hatred of evil? The apostle Paul wrote that Christians must never avenge themselves, instead leaving vengeance to "the wrath of God, for it is written, 'Vengeance is mine, I will repay, says the Lord'" (Rom. 12:19).

We'll find it difficult, however, to leave room for something we don't believe in. Often the quick flare-up of our wrath exposes our belief that we think we must do God's job for him.

This is one reason Christians do well to remember that the Bible promises a day when every knee will bow and every tongue confess that Jesus is Lord (Phil. 2:10–11). Some will bow to the beauty of God's grace willingly and joyfully, while others will be dropped to their knees by the blaze of God's righteous wrath. The book of Revelation speaks of a day when the ungodly—from the least to the greatest and from the poorest to the richest—will hide in clefts of rocks and call for boulders to crush them lest they face the wrath of him who is seated on the throne (Rev. 6:15–16).

A vibrant awareness of God's future punishment should not cause us to be less concerned about justice. Trust in God's ultimate justice should buttress our angst, guarding us against cynicism and despair. It's in this way we make sense of the imprecatory psalms, those passages of Scripture that cry out for God's justice against wrongdoers, verses such as Psalm 10:15 that asks God to "Break the arm of the wicked and evildoer." As we ask for God's hand to move, we remember we don't have to raise ours (Ps. 10:12).

We need to know that when all around our soul gives way, we may rest in the truth that Jesus will come again and no injustice will go without its full reckoning. To put this into the context of our cultural moment, we can say that the police officer who abuses a prisoner and the protestor who throws a brick at an officer both have views of God's wrath too small, not too big. As our cities burn, we need more preaching about God's wrath, not less.

When we forget God's wrath, we lose the urgency of missions. In John's gospel we read that anyone who believes in Jesus has eternal life, but for the one who does not believe and obey "the wrath of God remains on him" (John 3:36). The Bible often connects this reality of God's wrath toward sinners with urgency to preach the gospel. For example, after describing the judgement seat of Christ, the apostle Paul writes, "Therefore, knowing the fear of the Lord, we persuade others" (2 Cor. 5:11).

It's possible that all our Sunday school classes on evangelism fail to produce disciples who actually share their faith, not because the techniques are ineffective, but because our theology lacks teeth. Where there is no urgency the people perish.

I'm sure many in my church need to hear this, but I know I do too. I rarely feel the weight of the lost as I ought. Although, when God first tugged my heart toward pastoral ministry, I agonized over the thought of sinners going to hell. I remember visiting Navy Pier in Chicago, being surrounded by a hundred thousand other tourists. The weight of eternities felt palpable. I confess, my concern has diminished. Perhaps the grind of pastoral ministry and church administration have worn me down; perhaps I spend too much time with Christians and not the lost; perhaps I've capitulated to culture's passé view of hell; perhaps streams of Netflix have cooled my passion—perhaps all these and more.

Lord, help us. Lord, help me.

When we forget God's wrath, we lose the gospel. We can describe salvation as coming *from* God, *by* God, and *to* God. We are saved from God's wrath (1 Thess. 1:10) by God crushing his own Son in our place (Isa. 53:10; Rom. 3:25) so that he might bring us near (1 Pet. 3:18). Salvation is *from* God, *by* God, and *to* God.

When we forget God's wrath, we lose our understanding of God's love for us. Christians can marvel at the "kind of love the father has given to us, that we should be called children of God" *because* we know we "were by nature children of wrath" (1 John 3:1; Eph. 2:3).

One of the new Christians at our church will occasionally mention to me that for many years he didn't think he needed Christ in his life because his life was going so well. He had the sort of life people portray on Instagram. "If Jesus only makes a person's life better, what am I missing?" he thought.

I don't want to discount the many ways knowing Jesus makes one's life better. But knowing Jesus—the real Jesus—also makes life harder too. It is only as we preach about the holiness of God, the goodness of the law and the badness of our sin, about divine punishment and God's wrath, that the good news story of Jesus becomes actual good news to people who, admittedly, have a pretty good life without Christ. The dark backdrop of our sin and God's judgment allows the rays of gospel light to shine bright.

After A.W. Tozer stated that the most important thing about a person is what first comes to our minds when we think about God, he wrote, "We tend by a secret law of the soul to move toward our mental image of God."[2] In other words, our actions overflow from our understanding of God.

I wouldn't want the first thoughts my children have of their father to be of my anger. "Tell me about your father," someone

[2] Ibid.

asks them. "Oh, he's really angry." I don't want that. I want them to think first of my love, and God wants us to think first of his love. Yet to never preach about God's wrath, or to only sheepishly mention his anger over sin as though it were some unfortunate part of him, is to misunderstand God and his love. His anger burns because so does his love.

And our understanding of God might be the most important thing about us.

19

WHEN MINISTRY SUCCESS
BECOMES AN IDOL

When a House Built on Sand Went Splat

I remember exactly where I was when I lost interest in professional sports.[1]

In 1998 the World Cup was in France, and the player to watch was Michael Owen, starting forward for England. He was that country's youngest player ever to participate in a World Cup. I was sixteen. Michael Owen was eighteen. I was in my parent's basement in mid-Missouri. He was in the Stade de Toulouse in France. I played JV soccer, defense specifically, because I couldn't score. But Owen was scoring goals against the best players in the world. He was internationally famous. I was moderately popular in my high school.

The players were just as exciting as before I lost interest in professional sports; they hadn't changed. But somewhere along the way, as I grew up, things had changed for me. My

[1] This was my first published article by a major website, *The Gospel Coalition*, April 22, 2015, https://www.thegospelcoalition.org/article/when-ministry-success-becomes-an-idol/.

perspective had become twisted. I loved sports because one day I could be a star, or so I thought.

But at 16, I now had the sinking feeling that dreams long cultivated would not be harvested: in two years, I was not going to catch Owen.

All of this came flooding back to me a few months ago at the church office. In the stack of mail was *Christianity Today*. The cover story was titled "33 Under 33."[2] I just stared at the cover, as though opening it and skimming the pages would declare me guilty of something.

Temptation won.

The article celebrates, as you might expect, thirty-three leaders in Christianity (authors, pastors, musicians, entrepreneurs, political activists, and even a dancer) who are making a difference for Jesus. And they all have one thing in common (besides being on Twitter): they are all thirty-three years old or younger. I flipped the pages, and I stared at them—their super cool bios, trendy haircuts, and young faces. And they stared at me, all smiles. I frowned. It seemed, all over again, as though Michael Owen was scoring goals in France, and I was in my parent's basement.

Since this initial, deflating moment in the church office, I've had more time to think. Here's what was going on in my heart.

Anything can become an idol. The human heart has an astounding capacity to turn anything into an idol. To paraphrase Timothy Keller in *Counterfeit Gods*, when something, even a good thing, becomes an ultimate thing, then idolatry happens. Keller writes:

[2] Kate Shellnutt, "33 Under 33: Meet the Christian leaders shaping the next generation of our faith," *Christianity Today*, July 1, 2014, https://www.christianitytoday.com/ct/2014/july-august/33-under-33.html.

What is an idol? It is anything more important to you than God, anything that absorbs your heart and imagination more than God, anything you seek to give you what only God can give. . . . An idol is whatever you look at and say, in your heart of hearts, "If I have that, then I'll feel my life has meaning, then I'll know I have value, then I'll feel significant and secure." There are many ways to describe that kind of relationship to something, but perhaps the best one is *worship*.[3]

We can do this (idolatry) with just about anything. We can do it with soccer and athletics or with beauty and power. We can do it with career advancement, reputation in academia, political causes, or with family and children. We can do it with marriage or with singleness, profit or artistic expression.

"A-good-thing-turned-ultimate-thing" can even be true of Christian ministry success—the kind of Christian ministry success that appears in the glossy pages of *Christianity Today* calling to pastors from the stack of mail on the counter. In the CT article, Sam Hurd wrote:

Today, as American Christianity faces declining affiliation, intense public debates over religious freedom, changes in the family structure, and technological advances, millennial Christians have already picked up the baton. For this story, CT set out to find young believers who we think are leading today's church in key ways—and who embody what it will look like in the years to come.[4]

---

[3] Timothy Keller, *Counterfeit Gods: The Empty Promises of Money, Sex, and Power, and the Only Hope That Matters* (New York: Penguin, 2009), xvii–xviii.

[4] Shellnutt, "33 Under 33," *Christianity Today.*

The problem was not with the article; it was with my own heart. In other words, we should celebrate the provision of God and the faithfulness of his people, not bemoan our own anonymity. It was never about "us." It was never about me. Lord, forgive me for making the advancement of your kingdom about the advancement of mine.

God changes people. By the grace of God, people can, and do, change. Their desires can change; their worship can change. Through the gospel, people leave behind false gods and turn to the true God. Through Jesus, we can say that God "has delivered us from the domain of darkness and transferred us to the kingdom of his the beloved Son" (Col. 1:13).

On the morning I read "33 Under 33," the jealous urge was just a twinge, just a moment. Fifteen years ago, watching Owen in the World Cup, it was not just a twinge. Fifteen years ago, a sinkhole opened up, a foundation crumbled, and a house built on sand went splat. Fifteen years ago, there was not sorrow, but despair. Keller writes:

> There is a difference between sorrow and despair. Sorrow is pain for which there are sources of consolation. Sorrow comes from losing one good thing among others, so that, if you experience a career reversal, you can find comfort in your family to get you through it. Despair, however, is inconsolable, because it comes from losing an *ultimate* thing. When you lose the ultimate source of your meaning or hope, there are no alternative sources to turn to. It breaks your spirit.[5]

Since the time of Michael Owen, international phenom, versus Benjamin Vrbicek, JV peon, a decade and a half of life has

---

[5] Keller, *Counterfeit Gods*, x.

passed. In that time—only by God's grace—a new foundation has been laid with Christ as the cornerstone. That foundation cannot be shaken.

Start strong, finish strong. What matters in a race is how you finish. That's when they give the medals. I'm thankful for the young men and women celebrated by CT. I really am. I read their blogs and listen to their music. And now I'm praying for them the same thing I pray for myself: that we would finish strong.

Marriages can start well, pastorates can start well, and so can the Christian life. But consider Solomon in the Old Testament or Demas in the New Testament (Col. 4:14; Philem. 1:4; 2 Tim. 4:10). They seemed to start well, but they failed at what really counts: finishing well.

When we get to heaven, the true measure of every ministry will be evaluated, and faithfulness to Christ will be fully seen and rewarded. In light of that future, our highest aim should be to finish well, and hear in the end, "Well done, good and faithful servant." No matter our age, relative fame, or anonymity, may we all be able to say with Paul, "[We] have fought the good fight, [we] have finished the race, [we] have kept the faith" (2 Tim. 4:7).

20

HOW MUCH DOES A PASTOR WORK?

Wrestling with the Ambiguities of a Pastor's Timesheet

Having a conversation about how much a pastor works is like having a conversation about what a snowflake looks like: we can all draw a generic thumbnail sketch easily enough, but drawing the particulars comes with more difficulty.

I have no idea how much a pastor works even though I've been one for a decade. I'm sure a few pastors don't work enough, while many others work too much. But who decides what constitutes *too much* and *too little*? Who is the Goldilocks pastor who does just the right amount of work?

I did some reading recently about why pastors leave the ministry, and the authors cited an interesting study. In the 1950s the average pastor worked 69 hours a week, while in the 1990s the average pastor worked between 48–55 hours.[1] That's a significant drop, and a healthy one if you ask me. So, I made an Excel chart and plotted the trendline. If we extrapolate out, the average pastor in 2020 should have worked less than 40

---

[1] Dean R. Hoge and Jacqueline E. Wenger, *Pastors in Transition: Why Clergy Leave Local Church Ministry* (Grand Rapids: Eerdmans, 2005), 226.

hours per week, the global pandemic notwithstanding. Continuing the trend, we could suppose, then, by the time Jesus comes back pastors will only be working that one hour a week congregations always tease us about. And in heaven, they say, pastors will be out of jobs. But until then . . .

What Counts as Work? Deciding what counts as work and what doesn't count is not as obvious as you might think. Much of my job involves the kinds of activities you expect, the kinds of activities easier to track. Pastoring includes preparing and preaching sermons, counseling, administration, overseeing staff health, hospital visits, officiating weddings and funerals, leading and attending meetings, and so on.

But pastoral ministry sometimes involves less expected activities, like hosting a four-square tournament or "Youth Group Olympics" in your backyard; arranging the stage before and after a wedding and then vacuuming up all the glitter stuck in the carpet that fell from the bride's dress; washing church table cloths after a Wednesday memorial service luncheon; working on graphic design for the church welcome booklet, coffee mugs, and sermon posters; helping the guy who knocked on the front door of the church and just needs gas money to get home; talking for thirty minutes to a church member at a swimming pool on my off day when I was there to play with my kids; and occasionally shoveling icy-slush from the church walkway, plunging a clogged church toilet, and painting the church foyer; and so on. This is no campaign for sainthood; I've never touched a leper in Calcutta. But everything I listed comes from time-on-task in our church, the stuff of normal pastoring.

Some of these tasks fit in the typical nine-to-five, but many don't. And this is what makes it difficult to figure out how much, and how hard, we pastors work. Pastoring is more of a lifestyle job that goes with you everywhere you go, rather than one left at the office when you punch the clock. Thankfully, as our church has grown, the pastors at our church have a job description that looks less sporadic than my above list implies.

Recording Hours Worked. Rewind the clock with me about six years. At that time, I had been at my current church for just over a year. Perhaps in the hopes of doing a good job and perhaps because of my sinful inclinations to be a people-pleaser, I said "yes" to everything church members asked me to do. That's what it felt like, anyway. As you might expect, my schedule got out of control. Over one particular month, I remember working in the evenings five or six nights a week. You can't work both first *and* second shift for long stretches without developing problems. I was having problems.

I talked about this with one of our volunteer pastor-elders, and he encouraged me to prioritize my responsibilities. Also, per his encouragement, I began tracking every hour worked, though I wasn't happy about doing so. Up until that point in ministry, I had resisted tracking hours because in my former career as an engineer, I was required to track every half hour of work and submit a convoluted timesheet to HR at the end of each week. When I traded the calculator for a Bible, I never wanted to record my hours again.

But I had also resisted tracking the hours I worked in ministry because, as I said above, the nature of pastoral ministry makes tracking hours difficult. It can be hard to know if the time required to prepare your home to host a dinner for twenty people counts as "work," or if that extra time to clean your bathroom, mow your yard, and scrub your floor is part of owning a house. Sometimes it's not clear whether a dinner meeting was even a "work meeting" or whether it might be better described as just hanging out with friends. And after those twenty people leave your home, do the forty-five minutes it takes to clean up your house count as "work"? And if I bought the food for the meal with my church credit card, does my family get to eat the leftovers tomorrow?

(If you're a church member, please don't take these comments the wrong way, and don't think meanly of your pastor for asking these sorts of questions. If he is asking these sorts of questions, he's probably just trying to be faithful to the calling you've commissioned him to pursue.)

The best advice I have ever received about tracking pastoral hours came during a Q&A at a conference I attended years ago while in seminary. I don't even remember the name of the speaker, but I remember what he said when someone asked him how many hours a pastor should work and what constitutes work: *count it all and shoot for fifty hours.* "The volunteer pastors at your church probably have a salary job that requires them to work the standard forty hours a week, but in reality they probably work at least forty-five," he explained. "And then the church expects our volunteer pastors to give, on average, five hours a week to the local church, if not more. So, count it all and shoot for fifty. But be ready to do more on an occasionally busy week, just as your elder board is ready for more at work and church."

Perhaps this approach is too simple and arbitrary, but it's proved a handy guideline all these years later. I count the time to clean up my house after I host a dinner, and I count the time to attend a small group Bible study. I don't count my time to commute to work each day, but I do if I visit someone after hours at the hospital.

As much as I didn't want to track my hours for all the reasons listed above, I felt it was more important to know how much I was working, especially how many evenings a week I was away from home. So, per the suggestion of my friend, for the next two years I logged every half hour of work and found I averaged 46 hours a week and spent around 2–4 evenings a week away from home. That's a little light, according to the conference speaker's advice.

But *was it light*? We haven't counted it all yet.

What about "Writing Time"? This is where my specific calling in ministry further complicates the calculation of total work hours. Although it certainly does not make me a snowflake with a unique crystalline lattice, I am a pastor who also feels called by God to write. So, for most of the last seven years, the time before I took the role of managing editor for Gospel-Centered Discipleship, I treated my calling to write as a part-time but unpaid job. I don't often tell people I view it this way, but that is how I look at it. I do most of my writing early in the mornings between 5:30–7 a.m., and sometimes also on Friday afternoons from 2–4 p.m. Most weeks this adds up to about ten hours of writing on top of my day job.

Let me explain more of what I mean by calling my writing "unpaid." Writing has *not* been lucrative for me. Most years, when you add up all the expenses of hosting and maintaining my blog, writing articles for other websites, buying books for research, and paying for professional editing, any money I make from book royalties or the occasional article, does not make up for the money I lose. In accounting terms, my profits and losses are in the red.

I don't worry about this, though. I consider my writing ministry done unto the Lord. And I also look at it as an investment; maybe some year in the future, "losing a few thousand" will become "making a few thousand." But in the meantime, it feels obedient to keep working at my craft and growing in my ability to write words that help people find joy in God. Besides, I enjoy writing.

But here's the question: where do these extra 10 hours-per-week fit in relation to my 46 hours-per-week? Should I consider writing more of a hobby, in which case the hours don't count at all toward ministry hours? Or is this writing work so closely related to ministry that these hours do "count" as work? In math class, 10 plus 46 would equal 56, and since the case could be argued that with each blog post I write, the better I become at communicating Christian truth, which feels closely connected to the actual work of pastoring a church, and therefore these writing hours should be counted as regular work hours.

For years, I wrestled on my own with these questions. I won't bore you with all the internal iterations of how I parsed the details, but the angst proved lonely and, in the end, the wrong way to handle the ambiguity. The team of pastor-elders at our church have since helped me clarify how we, together, answer questions around what constitutes "company time" and what constitutes "hobby time," as well as the tricky financial aspects of writing. As formal and cumbersome as it might sound, we now have a signed writing agreement that, we think, benefits us both.

Why Am I Sharing This? I do not share these reflections because my confidence is high that I do everything the way a pastor should. I don't know what Enneagram number this makes me, but I'm the sort of pastor—the sort of person really—who often feels like I don't know if I'm doing the right thing even when I know I am, if that makes sense. So, I do the best I can to answer questions about work hours faithfully. And as I wrestle with how much to work and what to work on, I try to listen to my wife, the council of the pastors I work with, and friends and mentors who pastor different churches, as well as having an open, prayerful dialogue with the Lord about it all.

The reason I'm sharing all this now, is the hope that putting some of the ambiguities in the spotlight will help other pastors who wrestle with the same questions. Surely, I'm not the only one.

Also, I share these questions and the fact that I work about 46 hours a week to keep me accountable. It wouldn't be healthy or honoring to God for me to have worked 32 hours a week or to have worked 82 hours. Working 46 hours of "work-work" and 10 hours of "writing-work" seems to be the right amount for most weeks. The only time this balance doesn't seem to work is when I officiate a wedding. In wedding weeks I can't seem to figure out how to do less than 55 hours of work. And as much as I love officiating a beautiful wedding and preaching the gospel, I won't complain that when Jesus comes back, they will neither marry nor be given in marriage.

Despite what it might seem, this work and writing schedule has me with my family for almost every dinner, almost every breakfast, and almost every sporting event for my children, at least on the nights my wife and I don't have to "divide and conquer" because two or more of our children have sporting events in different places. I wish I made time to go on more dates with my wife, but I can't blame work for the infrequency. That's more a function of lack of effort on my part than it is too many evenings away for work.

The difficult part of pastoring on my family, it seems to me, is not the number of hours I work or the pay. The most difficult part for them is that too often I can't stop my mind from working even when I'm not working. I keep thinking about a certain marriage that is imploding, the sermon I've yet to write, and the parishioner who is mad at me—and vice-versa. At home I keep thinking about how to keep all the plates spinning at work. You can lead a pastor to Sabbath, but you can't make him rest.

To be sure, carrying the stress of work to one's home is not only a struggle for pastors, but we pastors should have less of an excuse; the theology we preach is the same theology we should live. Rest, at its core, is about faith. When we rest from our labor, when we forsake worry, when we take a nap, and when we play with Duplo Legos on the floor with our children, we declare that God is God, and he is the one who builds his church. Looked at this way, the atlas of anxiety a pastor too often carries is less a badge of honor representing his love for the church but more a demerit representing his lack of trust in God.

If you feel inclined to pray for me or to pray for your pastor, please do pray this: that pastors would work hard unto the Lord and not man, but when we are not working, we would not unduly trudge the work of the church home in our heads and hearts.

If there's a Microsoft Excel spreadsheet to figure out how to stop working when work is over, let me know. I could use it.

21

CONGREGATIONS OF BRUISED REEDS

Sturdy Hope for Fragile Followers

My parents adopted my cousin when she was a baby. While she slept in her crib, a man murdered her mother in the living room. I was about ten years old when we adopted her, and, for a time, I remember being afraid at night.

In this life there are so many ways to become bruised.

Sexual abuse has bruised many in our churches. The *New York Times* reported last year that in my own city of Harrisburg, Pennsylvania, the local diocese declared bankruptcy "to seek protection from creditors as it faces tens of millions of dollars in outstanding claims from people who were sexually abused by clergy members."[1] Of course the Catholic church has no monopoly on sexual abuse. At this point, we're all aware of the reporting by *Christianity Today* about Ravi Zacharias[2] and the

---

[1] Michael Levenson, "Pennsylvania Diocese, Facing More Abuse Claims, Files for Bankruptcy," *New York Times*, February 19, 2020, https://www.nytimes.com /2020/02/19/us/pennsylvania-church-sexual-abuse-victims.html.

[2] Daniel Silliman and Kate Shellnut, "Ravi Zacharias Hid Hundreds of Pictures of Women, Abuse During Massages, and a Rape Allegation, *Christianity Today*,

reporting done by the *Houston Chronicle* about the largest Protestant denomination in the world.[3]

But I don't think of abuse as mainly something "out there" done by and to others. Each week when I stand up to preach, I stand in front of women who have been sexually abused. Some I know about, and others I only suspect are there based on statistics. In her book *Talking Back to Purity Culture*, Rachel Joy Welcher quotes the statistic that "every two minutes, someone in the United States is sexually assaulted" and then adds, "If it is happening this often in America, it is happening to individuals in our churches."[4]

There are so many ways to become bruised. A ministry friend of mine used to be on staff at a large church. When he addressed with pointed questions the verbal and emotional abuse taking place by a leader, my friend was promptly dismissed and forced to sign an NDA, a non-disclosure agreement. In other words, they told my friend to take the money and shut up. Newly married, he had just bought a home in a new city. The firing process all happened so quickly. Years have now passed, and now that abusive pastor has since been fired, but my friend's heart has struggled to fully heal.

There are so many ways to become bruised. A few people in my church grew up with belligerent fathers. Now, every time a man raises his voice, they become disproportionally afraid. Others in my church have lost loved ones to suicide. I officiated the funeral of my grandfather who took his life. A dozen people

February 21, 2021, https://www.christianitytoday.com/news/2021/February/ravi-zacharias-rzim-investigation-sexual-abuse-sexting-rape.html.

[3] Lise Olsen and John Tedesco, "Abuse of Faith," *Houston Chronicle*, February 10, 2019, https://www.houstonchronicle.com/news/investigations/article/Southern-Baptist-sexual-abuse-spreads-as-leaders-13588038.php.

[4] Rachel Joy Welcher, *Talking Back to Purity Culture: Rediscovering Faithful Christian Sexuality* (Downers Grove, IL: InterVarsity, 2020), 108–109.

in my church suffer from chronic illness. And to one degree or another, all of us struggled over the last year with aspects related to Covid. There are just so many ways to become bruised. In fact, in Romans 8, we read that not only people but all creation groans under the futility it has been subjected to because of sin (Rom. 8:22).

Sometimes we don't even recognize our woundedness. If your temper roars out of control such that the people around you must walk on eggshells and handle you with mittens, then you're probably not as tough as you think. You're probably wounded, and for the sake of protection, you've become a snapping turtle with sharp teeth and a spiky shell so no one can ever know the real you.

What is God to do with wounded, bruised people like us? If you have a plastic grocery bag that gets a hole, you don't save it. You don't try to fix a disposable grocery bag. You throw it away and get a new one. Seven billion other, better grocery bags fill our world. Why duct tape a ripped and ruined one?

Thankfully, that is not how God treats us. His ways are not our ways. In Isaiah 42 we read about the compassion of our healer. "A bruised reed he will not break," Isaiah writes, "and a faintly burning wick he will not quench" (42:3).

Do not, however, be confused about the strength of our savior. When Isaiah writes that a bruised reed Jesus will not break, it's *not* that Jesus can't break a flimsy reed. God could break us as easily as a lion could crush a wounded hummingbird in his paw. God *could* crush us with no effort. Or he can set us down underneath him and protect us while we heal, which is what our savior does.

I've been competing in sports for the last thirty years, and over this time I've become a decent judge of how long a particular injury might keep an athlete sidelined. For example, I have a decent sense of how long it takes for a lightly sprained ankle to heal (three *weeks*, not three months) and how long it takes for broken ribs to heal (three *months*, not three weeks).

But how long does it take to heal from abuse? If a previous church treated a pastor badly, and that man shows up in our pews, has he suffered a *five-month* injury? And if a woman goes through the trauma of divorce or widowhood, has she suffered a *five-year* injury? I suppose the answer is, It depends.

Over the last decade of pastoral ministry, I have learned the time required to heal from abuse and other trauma is always longer than I would have guessed. I'll say it differently. When I was a less experienced pastor, I'd find myself looking at the spiritual equivalent of a broken arm and thinking, "Yeah, that will heal in a week or two," when in reality a compound fracture takes far longer to heal—*if* the bones ever do. I didn't guess wrong to be demeaning or triumphalist. In hindsight, I think I was just naïve.

Thankfully, the book of Isaiah does not treat the wounds of God's people lightly. As Isaiah writes later in the book, our Messiah was pierced for our transgressions, crushed for our iniquities, and with his wounds, we are healed (53:4). God does not treat the wounds of his people lightly. Our redemption came through a bloody cross. And whatever bruising remains unhealed in this life, God will fully heal in the next. The good work he begins in us, Paul writes, God will see to completion (Phil. 1:6)

22

COME TO ME ALL WHO
HAVE COVID WEARINESS

And I Will Give You Rest

My friend traded his pickup for a new one. I got a good look at it the other night. It's the kind of truck neighbors peer out the window to see as the rumbling engine idles in your driveway. You practically need a stepladder to climb up to the cab. The truck is a "dually," meaning the rear axle has two massive wheels on each side. The lug nuts on the front wheels have those spikes you see on tractor trailers. The truck is a beast made for towing. I'd say you could chain a redwood to the back, and it would yank out roots seven hundred years deep like I pull a seven-day-old weed. It's the kind of truck that makes you feel as though you could hitch the St. Louis Arch to the back and drag it like a horseshoe.[1]

Back in the day farmers had a way of hitching oxen together. They called wood and rope connecting system a yoke, which allowed the full force of two oxen to plow side by side. In parts

---

[1] This post was published during the thick of the Covid lockdown.

of the world, farming still proceeds in this way. Two healthy oxen might not budge a redwood, but oxen could work you and me to our death.

Jesus picks up this imagery in his familiar invitation in Matthew 11 to be yoked to him, to have rope and wood harnessed between our neck and his. Jesus promises, however, his yoke is easy and his burden is light. He promises this because, he says, "I am gentle and lowly." *Can you imagine being yoked to my friend's dually?* Nothing about that ride would be gentle.

The encompassing word *all* grabs my attention. Not some, not a few, not even many, but Jesus invites all who are heavy laden. All who feel hitched to a pickup too powerful, all who feel yoked to the servitude of sin, all who stagger under the weight of weariness, all who have rope burns across their necks and sun-scorched shoulders and arthritic aching knees from plowing, plowing, plowing. All may come to Jesus for rest.

Do you see yourself in the *all* or is the all only for someone else? As the Covid yoke lies heavy, will you come to Jesus for rest?

Mothers, will you come to Jesus for rest? You who are forced to put the *stay* in stay-at-home mothers, you may come to him for rest. Children follow you about the house as you run IT support and troubleshoot their iPads and Zoom calls and fix three meals a day with the food you could only get from a long line at the grocery store while wearing a mask.

Fathers, will you come to Jesus for rest? You work from home from when you wake until when you crash. Your family life and hobby life and work life and exercise life and church life ooze together. The compartments that contained the floods of craziness have collapsed. And you want to collapse as well.

Singles, will you come to Jesus for rest? Your social distancing feels more like acute social isolating, and you're starved for conversation, laughter, and a hug.

Students, will you come to Jesus for rest? Your college dorm room was cooler than your bedroom in your parent's house. Some of you celebrated your graduation with handmade caps and gowns and no other students or faculty. Others missed prom. Staying motivated to study when the weather warms was already difficult before Covid.

Health care workers, will you come to Jesus for rest? You labor risky hours over those who cough and sneeze and wonder if their fever or their morale will break first. The friends and family of your patients want to visit the hospital, but they are not permitted. So this familial labor also falls to you: not only must you take vitals and intubate but you must also hold the hand of those in intensive care.

Business owners and those who side-hustle to make ends meet, will you come to Jesus for rest? Your whole life you've achieved through your assertiveness, by showing up early and leaving late. Now—for reasons out of your control—you've been rendered passive. You can't forge ahead because you're not allowed. Now, homebound and without work, you wait for permission. Your spirit has restless leg syndrome.

Teachers, will you come to Jesus for rest? You lecture to a webcam and answer emails and walk the dog and grade papers all from your home classroom, which is far more of a home than a classroom.

The retired and elderly and all with compromised immune systems, will you come to Jesus for rest? Your friends cannot come to see you, and you feel more forgotten than before.

Government officials, will you come to Jesus for rest? Never have you made fewer people happy, and never have you shouldered more responsibility—responsibilities you never asked for or wanted. Weighing lives and livelihoods leaves dark circles under your eyes.

Pastors, will you come to Jesus for rest? Your church needs you. Your family needs you. You give and give and give. Ministry does not stop; it just changes venues. But when Jesus invites all, the all includes those who live to help others.

The flowing current of Covid sadness can drown the strongest swimmer. You might already be gasping for air. If you feel this way, come to Jesus. Pray to him. Read his word. Belong to his church. His grace can tow you from the mire better than any pickup. Come and enjoy the freedom found in being loved by the Savior, not controlled by a harsh slave master.

And if the waves of endless lockdown days break upon you, Jesus also wants you to tell a Christian friend. Send an email right now to a Christian who loves you and doesn't want to see you succumb to struggle. Your friends probably don't know how bad you feel; their own dose of quarantine might have made their gaze myopic. So, right now, send an honest text to a friend. Send the text if you feel the yoke of alcohol or porn or pain killers calling to you. Drive to the house of a friend and ask for prayer. Call your doctor if you feel the flood of depression rising.

A verse from an old hymn reads, "Come, ye weary, heavy laden, / lost and ruined by the fall; / if you tarry till you're better, / you will never come at all." For over two hundred and fifty years, these lyrics from Joseph Hart's hymn "Come, Ye Sinners, Poor and Needy" have extended the invitation of Christ to countless weary congregations.

Let the lyrics welcome you today.

You don't have to come with superior strength for Jesus to help you. You don't need to come with the dirt under your fingernails manicured. You can come with a Covid haircut. You can come to Christ without makeup and wearing your PJs. It may prick your pride, but you don't need to be business casual for Christ to help you. All you need is to know your need and the urgency that if you wait until you're better, you will never come at all.

23

SOMETIMES GOD JUST CLOSES DOORS

Our Afflictions Are Preparing for Us an Eternal Weight of Glory

For the last few years, my body has had a strange relationship with food. By strange, I mean terrible. Rather than providing nutrition, many foods provide me with small doses of poison. Which foods do this and in what amounts? I'm not sure. Actually, no one is sure—and that's the hardest part.

When the pain spikes and my stomach swells, I know I'm having a reaction. Most of the time, my only defense is to get some extra sleep and take more medicine, knowing the sickness will be gone in a few days. Sometimes, however, I worry something is really wrong, that I might be dying. I feel like Humpty Dumpty: all the king's horses and all the king's men—and all of the medical specialists and all of nature's holistic remedies— can't seem to get my digestive system working again. Over the last four years, I've accumulated a cabinet full of plastic bottles with strange labels, but found very little help.

As I've processed the nearly constant pain and inconvenience, I have been helped by Jared C. Wilson. He beautifully describes what it means to be broken and yet still loved by God.

He knows what it's like to let go of the rope we're all holding on to and let Jesus catch him. Wilson writes,

> I have a problem with all the "chase your dreams!" cheer-leading from Christian leaders. It's not because I begrudge people who want to achieve their dreams, but because I think we don't readily see how easy it is to conflate our dream-chasing with God's will in Christ.
>
> You know, it's possible that God's plan for us is littleness. His plan for us may be personal failure. It's possible that when another door closes, it's not because he plans to open the window, but because he plans to have the building fall down on you. The question we must ask ourselves is this: Will Christ be enough?[1]

This paragraph reflects a theme of Christianity that is often neglected in even our best churches: tomorrow might not be better than today.

Two things from Wilson's quote can be illustrated by looking briefly at the life of John the Baptist. First, the statement about littleness. John the Baptist said with reference to Jesus, "He must increase, but I must decrease" (John 3:30). John desired that Jesus would move into the spotlight instead of him, modeling for us the eternal beauty of littleness now.

Second, Wilson spoofs a common phrase in Christian lingo: that a closed door must mean another opportunity (a better opportunity!) will always arise. But it's possible that won't be the case—it wasn't for John. When God sent John to prison, he didn't get out. He was executed there (Matt. 14:1–12).

But before he was killed, John sent messengers to Jesus to ask if he was the Messiah, or if they should look for another

---

[1] Jared C. Wilson, *The Story of Everything: How You, Your Pets, and the Swiss Alps Fit into God's Plan for the World* (Wheaton: Crossway, 2015), 122.

(Matt. 11:1–3). Rather than nourishing his faith, the difficult circumstances of John's life were acting like poison, which then led him toward doubt and disillusionment. It just didn't seem like Jesus was doing the kinds of things he expected the Messiah would do. *If Jesus came to set captives free (Luke 4:18), then why am I still locked up?*

To be more blunt, in prison John was asking whether Jesus would be enough for him when he *actually did* decrease and it seemed he was going to die, and indeed would die. For, as Russell Moore put it, "The 'voice crying in the wilderness' ended up a severed voice box on a silver platter. The mouth that had spoken 'behold the Lamb of God who takes away the sin of the world' was taken out with the trash."[2]

And the question we often ask is similar to John the Baptist's question. Will Jesus be enough for us when one door closes and God doesn't open a window?

Yes, yes he will.

When you stand up for what's right and end up in jail (as was the case for John); when you have cancer; when you lose your job; when your house is robbed; when your parents get divorced; when you're sick and lying on the floor and your children ask, "Daddy, are you okay?" Jesus is still Jesus. And he will be enough for you.

When the apostle Paul repeatedly prayed for his difficulties to be taken away, God told him, "My grace is sufficient for you, for my power is made perfect in weakness" (2 Cor. 12:9). Elsewhere God reminds his people, "I will uphold you with my righteous right hand" (Isa. 41:10).

Today, if you are weak, know that Jesus is strong and he loves you dearly—even if you don't understand your own pain

---

[2] Russell Moore, *The Courage to Stand: Facing Your Fear without Losing Your Soul* (Nashville: B&H, 2021), 274.

and God's plan for it. Our afflictions are "preparing for us an eternal weight of glory beyond all comparison" (2 Cor. 4:17). Though the whole house falls down, our foundation in Christ will never crack.

24

DEAR TWITTER, I'M LEAVING
YOU FOR MY WIFE

Why I'm Done Participating (for Now) in the Insanity

I might have to walk this decision back, but for now, I'm leaving Twitter. And Facebook. And Instagram.

The latter two accounts were killed more as collateral damage than being directly engaged as enemy combatants.

I suppose it's probably more accurate to say I'm simply inducing a coma for my social media accounts than it is to say that I'm leaving them or even killing them—but death sounds more dramatic, and dramatic seems to get more attention, so let's just say I killed them.

I'll tell you a few of the reasons why I'm quitting Twitter, even though I won't presume that one pastor's reasons for abandoning Twitter have any interest to you. Basically, I joined and remained on Twitter for only a handful of reasons. I liked seeing what my friends from around the world were up to, most of whom are fellow pastors. And I liked seeing what my Christian heroes were up to—again, mostly pastors and authors. I also liked having a vague sense of what was going on more broadly in Christianity. Finally, I supposed that being on Twitter helped me share my books and articles. All of these—the friends, the heroes, the news-worthy events, the writing—were beneficial to me, even sources of joy.

I started to realize, though, that the underbelly of "Christian Pastor Twitter"—you know, all the snark, all the trolling, all the assuming-the-worst, all the myopic nitpicking—might not be the underbelly. The worst part of Twitter might actually be the whole pig—the head, the body, the arms, the legs, the snout, the curly tail, and not just the underbelly. The exception had become the rule. In fairness, Twitter has probably been this way for a good while, but my experience with Twitter had, at least until recently, remained primarily positive.

But then in the middle of March 2021 came a string of what I can only call insanity.

There was a lousy but virally shared review of the book *Gentle and Lowly* by Dane Ortlund. If you missed the review, you are better for it.[1] A book reviewer managed to misread an excellent book written by a hero of mine, and the review got a lot of people worked up, including me.

Then there was the shooting at the massage parlors in Atlanta, which seemed to cause several social commentators to offer bizarre and irresponsible hot takes. For example, within days of the shootings, some suggested that Christian teaching about sex caused the shooting because the shooter was a member of a church. An article in the *New York Times* spun it this way.[2] One of my former seminary professors even took the opportunity to slander a thoughtful, biblical organization, saying

[1] The review of *Gentle and Lowly* that appeared on a popular website of an evangelical ministry appears to have been removed.

[2] Ruth Graham, "Atlanta Suspect's Fixation on Sex Is Familiar Thorn for Evangelicals," *New York Times*, Published March 20, 2021, https://www.nytimes.com/2021/03/20/us/evangelical-sex-addiction-atlanta-suspect.html.

that the organization had "radicalized" the shooter.[3] That accu-
sation is absurd—and again, slanderous. I know I shouldn't care
as much as I do, but I write for the organization that he slan-
dered, and that organization has blessed me and our church in
a thousand tangible ways. It seems wildly reckless to connect
with a thick, straight line the worst version of Christian teaching about sex—teaching that would be better labeled as *un*-
Christian teaching—and say that it is because of Christian
teaching that women are dead. This connection, at best, is a
thin correlation and certainly not causation.

That same week another hero of mine, Collin Hansen,
tweeted about what a rough week it had been on social media
and included a link to the new book he cowrote about hope. I'm
so glad he wrote the book. What person couldn't use more hope
in our anxious age? But when I clicked to see the comments
underneath Hansen's tweet, it seemed to me, people salivated
at the opportunity to tear him down. It was like Hansen and The
Gospel Coalition (TGC) where he works were the source of all
the world's problems. One person likened Hansen to an arsonist
who feigns confusion standing before the ashes of the house he
just torched. In other words, the Twitter commentator was saying that Hansen and the goons at TGC caused the terrible week
on social media by years spent cultivating the toxic Twitter environment, so hence he shouldn't be so perplexed by his
handiwork.

Speaking of culpability, I should insert a note here I haven't
mentioned yet. I know that I am culpable for my Twitter feed.
The specifics of all the social media algorithms may remain
opaque, but the principle is readily known: *the more you click,
the more you get.* And I certainly got. For every doofus Twitter
comment I clicked, I got ten more comments in my feed. My

---

[3] I am intentionally not footnoting the source of this comment.

eyes were reaping the seeds I had sown with my thumbs. Forgive me, Lord.

This reaping led to more and more reaping. Controversies I didn't know existed were foisted upon me. And the "news" I had tried to remain vaguely aware of started to become the headlines I'd rather be completely unaware of. "Beth Moore Leaves the SBC." "James White Said Something Provocative and Made People Mad." "Somewhere Someone with White Skin Said Something Racist."

As an evangelical pastor, I began to feel like each time I opened Twitter, I stood trial for all the dumb things fringe evangelicals had done. To open Twitter was to be prosecuted by the mob. And mobs don't do nuance well.

It's not that I don't care about Beth Moore and the like, but I am a pastor of a church with plenty of our own problems, and all of our church problems I care about far more than the problems I didn't start and I can't fix. Indeed, one day I will be held accountable to God, not for whether I engaged in the latest Twitter storm but whether I loved the sheep of my flock. And while we're on the subject of divine accountability and moral imperatives, I also have a large family, and they are my first pastoral priority. Each time I turn around, my children grow an inch or two and seem to be one step closer to walking out our front door and onto a college campus. Time flies when you have toddlers and teenagers in the same house.

Rod Dreher argues in his popular book *The Benedict Option*[4] that Christians should retreat to the places where we can have meaningful influence; in a sense, we should become Benedictine monks on Noah's ark. Conservative Christians, he would say, must become those who actually have something to

---

[4] Rod Dreher, *The Benedict Option: A Strategy for Christians in a Post-Christian Nation* (New York: Sentinel, 2017).

conserve (re: godliness) and spend our time conserving it. I read the book a few months ago and found it insightful even if I don't take his conclusions to be the only, or even the best, option for Christians. But perhaps Dreher's arguments worked on me more subtly than I realized. Today, I feel content to let the Twitter dumpster fire burn while I retreat to play with my kids and love my wife and pastor my church.

This gets to the real issue. In addition to all the drama, Twitter had become an all-consuming time drain, devouring every bit of my mental rest and human interaction. Do I really need to open Twitter while I walk upstairs to grab my running shoes? Do I need to recheck when I walk down the stairs to see what I missed during the thirty seconds it took to find my shoes? Do I need to check Twitter with one hand and brush my teeth and comb my hair with the other? Do I need to check Twitter as I walk from my car to the office in the morning and then again while I warm my coffee in the office microwave? No, no, no, and no. And more importantly, do I need to multitask when I talk with my wife? Same answer.

When I tweeted that I was leaving Twitter, I wrote, "If you want to reach out to me, send me a *text* message." A few days later I checked the comments, and someone had asked, "Do you mean a *direct* message?" Actually, no. I did mean text message. If you have my cell phone, let's keep in touch.

So, Dear Twitter, for all these reasons, I'm leaving you for my wife. And for my family. And for my joy. Your tidal wave of trash and the general social media sea of cesspool finally rose so high and crashed so hard on my little island oasis of joy where I visited with my friends and heroes that I'm going to float away.

Maybe one day the violent waters will recede, I'll get off my ark, and we can be friends again.

25

MY HEART IS FULL

A Miniature Memoir after Five Years of Ministry in One Church

Pastor and author John Piper has said that "God will hide from you much of your fruit [from your ministry efforts]. You will see enough to be assured of his blessing, but not so much as to think you could live without it."[1]

I've found this to be true. Most of the time I hear enough encouragement in ministry that I don't want to quit. And most of the time I tend not to hear so much encouragement as to become proud. But the receiving of encouragement is not always so balanced in the short run. Receiving encouragement is a lot like gaining and losing weight. When you are, on the whole, losing weight, you still gain weight each time you eat, even if the total calories you burn create a weekly deficit. And when, on the whole, you're gaining weight, each time you exercise or do any movement or make no movement as you sleep, your body burns calories. Encouragement and discouragement in ministry are similarly in constant flux.

[1] John Piper, *The Supremacy of God in Preaching* (Grand Rapids: Baker, 2004 edition), 25.

It's fair to say that encouragement didn't come my way often when I first arrived at my current church. Early on, I never really wanted to leave, nor did I feel like anyone especially wanted me to leave. But I sort of had this sense that if I did leave, no one would miss me too much. People didn't love or hate my pastoring; they seemed indifferent. That might be overstating things, but it accurately describes how I felt.

I'm not sure of all the reasons I perceived these feelings of indifference. In hindsight, I believe the largest contributing factor was my change in role. At my former church, encouragement dripped into my inbox like it was hooked up to an IV bag, potent and steady. But at my last church, I was an associate teaching pastor, not a senior teaching pastor. Church members like rooting for an associate pastor, especially if he's trying hard and keeps improving. I'd preach an okay-ish sermon one week, but then a few months later I might preach a sermon that was a little better than just okay. People would let me know ways I had improved. They'd show me notes they took during the sermon, and even a month later send text messages about how the sermon was still ministering to them. Eventually, I preached a few sermons that could almost be considered good by associate pastor standards. A few times near the end I might have even preached well. That was fun. Again, the congregation rooted for me. Who doesn't want an underdog to win?

When I came to Community Evangelical Free Church, no longer an associate teaching pastor but a senior teaching pastor, someone also pulled the IV out of my inbox. It's not that anyone ever said this outright, but it almost felt like people were thinking, *Hey, you're a senior teaching pastor now; we sort of expect your sermons to be good, and the same goes for your counseling, discipleship, Bible knowledge, administration, and everything else you do.*

For whatever deficit of encouragement there was in the first few years—whether it was an actual deficit or it was just perception, only the Lord knows—I certainly know now that my church is rooting for me. My church gave me a big dose of encouragement when we celebrated my five-year anniversary. A few members of the original pastoral search team, staff, elders, my small group, and a few other friends, gave up an evening to share ways that my wife and I have blessed them through our ministry here. They even prayed over us. My heart is full.

In one note, a dear friend wrote, "I see you in the trenches week in and week out wrestling with the Scriptures, honing your preaching craft, writing for the edification of God's people, centering (and re-centering) your work, ministry, and family on the gospel. . . . Over the last five years you've made gospel-centeredness tangible."

That note and the other notes hold more life-giving encouragement than I feel comfortable sharing here. I don't want my reflections to be considered self-serving. But one thing stood out as people around the room shared: the wide cross-section of life that pastoral ministry occupies. For one couple, I had officiated the weddings of two of their daughters. For another couple, I had visited them in the hospital while they sat beside the bed of a dying parent, once for a father and once for a mother. I had also prayed with new mothers and fathers in hospitals when their children were born. With others, we'd shared tears and prayers and pans of brownies in homes during countless small group meetings. And all of them had endured my preaching. Speaking of preaching . . .

My best friend, Mike, had a raffle of sorts to see who could guess how many sermons I had preached during my first five years. My co-pastor and I alternate preaching, so it wasn't difficult to do a little math and make a decent guess. My guess didn't count, but I thought it might have been around one hundred and ten, which turned out to be a little high. In a few seasons, like the year we renovated a building, my preaching frequency slowed a bit. The answer was one hundred and four sermons in the first five years, which amounts to something like four-hundred thousand words. That's a lot of words.

Do you remember those arcade games with a mechanical bar that slides back and forth, continually nudging a huge stack of coins resting on a shelf? You play the game by dropping in coins and hoping the mechanical bar will nudge the stack in such a way that some eventually fall off the ledge. That's often how I think about preaching and pastoral ministry. Preaching is a series of tiny nudges. There are the granular nudges in four-hundred thousand individual words and the aggregate nudges in one hundred and four completed sermons. With most nudges, nothing seems to happen. So, in faith a pastor reloads for another sermon and again another nudge.

And again.

And again.

Then sometimes the nudges connect. Change happens. God helps and heals people. I'm thankful my church cared enough about me to show me the fruit from a few of my ministry nudges.

My heart is full.

PUBLICATION NOTE

Each essay was originally published in the following place:

1   "Bending the Covid Bow of Bronze"
    EFCA Now, website of *The Evangelical Free Church of America*

2   "The Day That Darrin Died"
    BenjaminVrbicek.com

3   "Pastor, Why Aren't You Preaching about What's Happening?"
    Gospel-Centered Discipleship (originally a two-part series)

4   "Redeeming Pastoral Ambition"
    9Marks

5   "Spring Loaded Camming Devices and the Expository Sermon"
    EDA Move, the website of *The Eastern District of The Evangelical Free Church of America*

6   "When My Church Was Washed with Butter"
    The Gospel Coalition

7   "Ministry Morning, Noon, and Night"
    Fathom Mag

ABOUT THE AUTHOR

Benjamin Vrbicek and his wife Brooke have six children. Benjamin enjoys reading, wrestling with his children, dating his wife, eating at Chipotle, and riding his bicycle in the early hours of the morning.

He earned a degree in mechanical and aerospace engineering from the University of Missouri and a masters of divinity from Covenant Theological Seminary in St. Louis, Missouri. He is the lead pastor at Community Evangelical Free Church in Harrisburg, Pennsylvania and the managing editor for Gospel-Centered Discipleship. He is coauthor of *Blogging for God's Glory in a Clickbait World* and author of *Don't Just Send a Resume* and *Struggle Against Porn*. He blogs regularly at his blog, Fan and Flame, and has also written for The Gospel Coalition, Desiring God, For The Church, 9Marks, Gospel-Centered Discipleship, and Christianity Today.